WHERE THE WORLD MEETS TO PRAY

Daniele Och
UK editor

INVITATIONAL
INTERDENOMINATIONAL
INTERNATIONAL

33 LANGUAGES
Multiple formats are available in some languages

 Ministries

15 The Chambers, Vineyard
Abingdon OX14 3FE
+44 (0)1865 319700 | brf.org.uk

Bible Reading Fellowship is a charity (233280)
and company limited by guarantee (301324),
registered in England and Wales

ISBN 978 1 80039 388 2

Originally published in the USA by The Upper Room® **upperroom.org**
US edition © 2025 The Upper Room, Nashville, TN (USA). All rights reserved.
This edition © Bible Reading Fellowship 2024
Cover photo by vadimmarkin/pexels.com

Acknowledgements

Scripture quotations marked with the following abbreviations are taken from the
version shown. Where no abbreviation is given, the quotation is taken from the same
version as the headline reference.

NIV: The Holy Bible, New International Version (Anglicised edition) copyright © 1979,
1984, 2011 by Biblica. Used by permission of Hodder & Stoughton Publishers, an
Hachette UK company. All rights reserved. 'NIV' is a registered trademark of Biblica.
UK trademark number 1448790.

NRSV: The New Revised Standard Version Updated Edition. Copyright © 2021
National Council of Churches of Christ in the United States of America. Used by
permission. All rights reserved worldwide.

CEB: copyright © 2011 by Common English Bible.

KJV: the Authorised Version of the Bible (The King James Bible), the rights in which
are vested in the Crown, are reproduced by permission of the Crown's Patentee,
Cambridge University Press.

A catalogue record for this book is available from the British Library

Printed and bound in the UK by Zenith Media NP4 0DQ

How to use *The Upper Room*

The Upper Room is ideal in helping us spend a quiet time with God each day. Each daily entry is based on a passage of scripture and is followed by a meditation and prayer. Each person who contributes a meditation seeks to relate their experience of God in a way that will help those who use *The Upper Room* every day.

Here are some guidelines to help you make best use of *The Upper Room*:

1 Read the passage of scripture. It is a good idea to read it more than once, in order to have a fuller understanding of what it is about and what you can learn from it.
2 Read the meditation. How does it relate to your own experience? Can you identify with what the writer has outlined from their own experience or understanding?
3 Pray the written prayer. Think about how you can use it to relate to people you know or situations that need your prayers today.
4 Think about the contributor who has written the meditation. Some users of *The Upper Room* include this person in their prayers for the day.
5 Meditate on the 'Thought for the day' and the 'Prayer focus', perhaps using them again as the focus for prayer or direction for action.

Why is it important to have a daily quiet time? Many people will agree that it is the best way of keeping in touch every day with the God who sustains us and who sends us out to do his will and show his love to the people we encounter each day. Meeting with God in this way reassures us of his presence with us, helps us to discern his will for us and makes us part of his worldwide family of Christian people through our prayers.

I hope that you will be encouraged as you use *The Upper Room* regularly as part of your daily devotions, and that God will richly bless you as you read his word and seek to learn more about him.

Helping to pay it forward

As part of our Living Faith ministry, we're raising funds to give away copies of Bible reading notes and other resources to those who aren't able to access them any other way, working with food banks and chaplaincy services, in prisons, hospitals and care homes.
If you've enjoyed and benefited from our resources, would you consider paying it forward to enable others to do so too?

Make a gift at **brf.org.uk/donate**

thank
y♥u
for all your support

Remaining open

I am about to do a new thing; now it springs forth; do you not perceive it? I will make a way in the wilderness and rivers in the desert.
Isaiah 43:19 (NRSV)

The season of Lent commemorates Jesus' 40 days in the wilderness and offers us an opportunity to prepare for the new reality that Jesus' resurrection makes possible. In this issue of *The Upper Room*, writers describe a variety of wilderness experiences: surgeries and health crises, financial struggles, retirement, moving to new places. Each of these situations is marked by uncertainty and often a sense of isolation. The challenge in wilderness experiences is to remain open and attentive to God's creative presence.

How do we remain open, alert for opportunities to experience the 'new thing' God is doing in our lives and in the world? Our writers offer a range of practices that help us perceive and share God's love, including gratitude journals, intercessory prayer, daily scripture study, calling individuals by name, careful listening and small acts of compassion. I pray that in this season, we will find the practices that open our hearts to all the opportunities God offers, so that we may proclaim to the world the hope and grace revealed in the resurrection.

Lindsay Gray
Editorial director

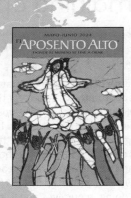

Spanish edition

Writers featured in this issue of *The Upper Room*:

Norma Gabriela Stieben (Argentina)
María de los Ángeles Vélez (Chile)
Sister Confianza del Señor (Honduras)
Roberto Rentería (México)
Estela Baldeón (Perú)

Gifts to the international editions of
The Upper Room help the world meet to pray.
upperroom.org/gift

The editor writes...

Many have undertaken to draw up an account of the things that have been fulfilled among us, just as they were handed down to us by those who from the first were eye witnesses and servants of the word. With this in mind… I too decided to write an orderly account for you.
Luke 1:1–3 (NIV)

Imagine being one of the gospel writers. You are setting out to write an account of the most extraordinary life of Jesus of Nazareth. Where do you begin? How do you put into words who Jesus is and all that he did? As one gospel writer says, the world may well not have enough room to fit the books that could be written on the subject (see John 21:25). I find it hard enough sometimes to compose a few paragraphs for an inconsequential email; how do you go about penning a narrative of the life of 'the Son of the Most High' (Luke 1:32)?

At the beginning of Luke's gospel, we get a little glimpse of how he began to tell the story of Jesus. Luke says he decided to write his 'orderly account' based on the stories 'handed down to us by those who from the first were eye witnesses and servants of the word'. That is, he sifted through the numerous accounts from various people who saw and heard what Jesus did and said, and what that meant for them, and he used those accounts to build up a picture of the life of Jesus – who he is and what he is like.

I like to think that *The Upper Room* helps us to do the same thing. I certainly do not claim that the meditations in here carry the same weight of inspiration as the writings of the evangelists or any other biblical author. But I like to think that, as you read the various accounts of the ways that people around the world have met with Jesus and put their trust in him, their meditations help us to better know who Jesus is and what he is like. Reading *The Upper Room* is, of course, no substitute for reading the Bible itself, especially the gospels. But I pray that as you read the following pages – together with the Bible – you may, to quote Luke once again, 'know the certainty of the things you have been taught' (1:4).

Daniele Och
UK editor

A new beginning

Read Romans 12:1–2
If anyone is in Christ, the new creation has come: the old has gone, the new is here!
2 Corinthians 5:17 (NIV)

I glanced out my front window, and the street was quiet. It was just another day. Last night, however, was much different. We heard the whistle and pop of exploding fireworks, the cheers of excited children and the shouting of jubilant well-wishers ushering in the New Year.

For many, the start of a new year is a time for resolutions, marking a new beginning and starting with a clean slate. One might give up a bad habit, begin a new exercise regimen, eat healthier foods, mend a broken relationship or improve some other aspect of their daily life. All this is done in the hope of having a happier, better and more fulfilled life.

Every New Year's Eve reminds me of my own new beginning in 1967 as a young teen. My new beginning wasn't a resolution to change one or two undesirable traits but complete repentance, and it transformed my life. The Lord Jesus Christ did all the work. I became a new creation. What joy there is in serving Jesus!

While salvation is wonderful, it doesn't stop there. As Christians we must continue to grow in faith. We must be diligent in reading and following God's word. Let us be examples to those around us and glorify God with our lives.

Prayer: *Dear Lord, help us to grow in our relationship with you. May others see our good works and glorify your name. Amen.*

Thought for the day: When I spend time in God's word, I nourish my soul.

Thomas Davis (Ontario, Canada)

Honest anger

Read Psalm 103:1–8

The Lord is compassionate and gracious, slow to anger, abounding in love.
Psalm 103:8 (NIV)

My mother was my hero and my cheerleader. But then because of alcohol, she was in and out of my life. I remember watching my mother slowly be consumed by her addiction. During the progression of my mother's disease, I was so upset with God that I stopped praying. One day, full of rage, I broke my silence to yell at God for what was happening. I was surprised to sense that God was listening patiently to me, and I began to talk with God more and more each day.

Trusting God during times of sorrow and suffering is difficult. I still have days where it is hard to get out of bed or get into my daily routine without feeling as if I'm just going through the motions. Starting my mornings with prayer and meditation on scripture helps to keep me focused on the day ahead. My heartache remains, but with time and God's help, the pain of losing parts of my relationship with my mum has ceased and my relationship with God has grown.

Loss in relationships can bring sadness, confusion and anger. But my relationship with my mum has taught me that God is with us – through any and all situations. God can handle our anger.

Prayer: *O Lord, only you know how deep our hurt is and how long we have lived with it. Help us to release our anger and let go of our bitterness. Thank you for loving us unconditionally. Amen.*

Thought for the day: I can be honest with God, trusting that God will transform my heart.

Lauren Walker (Texas, USA)

In everything

Read Isaiah 30:15–18

'In repentance and rest is your salvation, in quietness and trust is your strength, but you would have none of it.'
Isaiah 30:15 (NIV)

When I was a child, I often saw Javan munia birds in rural rice fields. Farmers consider these birds pests because they eat the rice. Sometimes farmers shoot at the flock with air rifles. Interestingly, when the birds hear the shots, they panic and bump into each other or get stuck in tree branches, causing their own demise.

When sudden change happens, sometimes I'm just like those birds. I react poorly out of shock and panic, and I run into problems. Once when I heard a rumour, I panicked and reacted but later realised the rumour was incorrect. Likewise, often when I heard good news, I would get too excited and make snap judgements that I ultimately regretted.

Then I read Isaiah 30:15: 'In quietness and trust is your strength.' Instead of putting panic and emotion first, I learned that it is better to remain calm and trust God. As Proverbs 19:2 says, 'Hasty feet miss the way!' So I learned to be still, try to think clearly and pray. I learned to trust that even if I stumbled, God would not allow me to fall.

Prayer: *Dear God, help us not to follow our panic but rather to trust you in all circumstances. Amen.*

Thought for the day: In the face of adversity I will trust in God's quiet strength.

Ary Cahya (Central Java, Indonesia)

Making room

Read Matthew 3:1–12

'Repent, for the kingdom of heaven has come near.'
Matthew 3:2 (NIV)

There's something about the new year that feels full of hope and possibility. The anticipation of something new gives me the desire to clear out the clutter and create space – both physically and mentally – for what the year will bring.

John the Baptist was called to prepare Israel for the coming Messiah. He preached a message of repentance, urging people to turn their hearts towards God by clearing their lives of sin and making room to receive Christ. We, too, are called to prepare for Christ because God has work for us to do! We can prepare our hearts by repenting of our sin and giving our lives fully to God – clearing out the clutter that keeps us from following the Lord wholeheartedly.

If we want to see God at work in our lives, we must make room for God's presence. What clutter do we need to clear from our habits, our schedules or our hearts to create room for God's Spirit to move in? God wants to begin something new in us, so let's anticipate that gift by making room for it!

Prayer: *O God, show us what we need to clear from our lives to make more room for you. Amen.*

Thought for the day: Today I will create space for the Lord to work.

Sarah Bradstreet (New York, USA)

A faithful steward

Read Luke 16:1–15

It is required of stewards that they be found trustworthy.
1 Corinthians 4:2 (NRSV)

I was serving as a youth usher at our church. One Sunday morning during the service, as part of my duties, I hurried to the back of the church to gather the bags for the collection of the offering. I put my hand into one of the bags to check if it was empty. Lo and behold, I found a brand new 1,000 Nigerian naira note. I was tempted to take it and keep it for myself. But by the grace of God I was able to overcome the temptation and prove myself to be a faithful steward.

Jesus told his disciples: 'Whoever is faithful in a very little is faithful also in much, and whoever is dishonest in a very little is dishonest also in much' (Luke 16:10). To be a faithful steward of God's gifts, one must be honest, God-fearing and loyal – not given to service for the sake of appearances and self-will. This applies not only to our activities and duties within the church but to our day-to-day lives and activities within our families, neighbourhoods, schools and workplaces. God blesses our faithful stewardship.

Prayer: *Dear God, help us to be faithful to you in every aspect of our lives. Amen.*

Thought for the day: I can glorify God by being a faithful steward.

Gideon Idowu (Oyo, Nigeria)

The unexpected

Read Matthew 2:1–12

*'My thoughts are not your thoughts, neither are your ways my ways,'
declares the Lord.*
Isaiah 55:8 (NIV)

The magi travelled far looking for 'the one who has been born king of
the Jews' (Matthew 2:2). They sought him in Jerusalem, but King Herod
sent them to Bethlehem, which is where the chief priests and teachers
of the law said the Messiah was to be born. There they found the baby
Jesus, not in a palace but in a house, with his mother. Had I been one of
them, I might have been disillusioned, but scripture gives no indication
that they were disappointed by the humble scene.

When God's answers are not what we expect, it can be disappoint-
ing. Our church experienced this during the long process of finding a
new senior pastor. The church elders scheduled guest preachers for a
couple of months and then arranged for an interim pastor to serve for
a year while a search was conducted. But two weeks before the interim
pastor was to arrive, he informed us that he would not be coming. We
were back to square one!

This was not what we had expected, but it was a wonderful opportunity to practise trusting God. God's answers may not be what we expect,
but they are always perfect. Like the magi, we can receive them with joy.

Prayer: *Dear Lord, thank you for your awesome power and for your
perfect, unexpected answers to our prayers. Amen.*

Thought for the day: I can trust that God's ways are always best.

Lisa Stackpole (Wisconsin, USA)

Garden grace

Read John 15:1–9

'I am the vine; you are the branches. Those who abide in me and I in them bear much fruit.'
John 15:5 (NRSV)

One of my favourite memories is of my dad sitting on a fresh bed of pine straw in the middle of his rose garden. With an unlit pipe in his mouth, he would spend hours clipping, spraying and caring for his rose bushes. He grew the most beautiful fragrant roses imaginable. Dad loved to take them to work and put them on all the office desks. He also spread them throughout our house. I remember the rich fragrance of roses throughout our home, and every time I smell a rose, I think of Dad.

The problem with rose gardening is that rose stems have thorns. Every now and then Dad got pricked, and then he might say something I won't repeat here. Still, he continued to love and care for his roses.

Through our scripture passage I understand Christ as the gardener in our lives. For me, the fruit is God's grace growing within us and also allowing us to make a difference in the lives of others. Yet, like rose stems, our lives have thorns. Sometimes thorns prick me pretty good, and sometimes my thorns prick others as well. I find I need some time each day to focus on God's grace in Christ. Jesus invites us to abide in his love, and I hope we can all find our own unique ways to do that each and every day.

Prayer: *Dear God, thank you for caring for us with the attentiveness of a gardener. Help us to abide in your love so that we may show grace to others. Amen.*

Thought for the day: Focusing on God's love shows me how to extend grace to others.

Stephen Smith (Alabama, USA)

Eyes on God

Read Psalm 34:1–7
Your word is a lamp for my feet, a light on my path.
Psalm 119:105 (NIV)

My husband was experiencing one illness after another. Before he had time to recover from open-heart surgery, he had to undergo another operation. A few weeks after that operation, he became ill and needed to be hospitalised again. I reached out to God in prayer and asked for help through this ordeal. But I still felt anxious and helpless. Overwhelmed with fear, I began to doubt and to ask where God was during all these trials.

The next day I opened my Bible for my daily devotions and came across 2 Chronicles 20 and decided to read the chapter. As I read, verse 12 stood out to me. Faced with a crisis, King Jehoshaphat cried out to God: 'We do not know what to do, but our eyes are on you' (2 Chronicles 20:12). I identified with his heartfelt prayer, and I made it my own. I needed to keep my eyes on God and trust God. A peace and quiet came over me then, and I knew that God was present in our situation.

No matter what happens in our lives, God is with us – even when we do not realise it. And when we call upon God in our distress, we can trust that God hears us and cares about us.

Prayer: *Dear God, when we are confronted by trials, lead us to the guidance you have provided in your word. Amen.*

Thought for the day: When I feel afraid and in doubt, I can find comfort in God's word.

Rita Alexander (Free State, South Africa)

How unfair!

Read Matthew 5:43–48

'Love your enemies and pray for those who persecute you.'
Matthew 5:44 (NIV)

'I can't believe how much trouble that woman is causing,' I complained to my husband. 'She tries to get her finger in everything and is such a gossip, stirring up trouble wherever she goes.'

My husband listened carefully to what I was saying and generally agreed with me. But he asked me to consider something. He pointed out that Jesus loved her just as much as he loved me. That just blew my mind. *How unfair!* I thought. I was behaving well, and she wasn't.

I prefer my husband to be supportive by always taking my side. I don't like it when he's reasonable and makes sense, requiring me to course-correct! He did give me a little help, though, by suggesting that I pray for eyes to see that woman as God does. Slowly, I began to open up to the idea. God began to show me that she was created in the divine image, just as I was. That alone is worthy of my respect.

Jesus challenges us to love those who are difficult to love. It's easy to love those who agree with us. But God has called us to a higher standard. While we were still sinners, God loved us anyway. I remain a work in progress. With God by my side through prayer, I am learning that all persons are worthy of my respect.

Prayer: *Dear God, thank you for loving us. Help us to see everyone as worthy of love and respect. Amen.*

Thought for the day: God loves my enemies as much as God loves me.

Carol McCracken (Alabama, USA)

Hidden in plain sight

Read Isaiah 43:16–21

Because of the Lord's great love we are not consumed, for his compassions never fail. They are new every morning; great is your faithfulness.

Lamentations 3:22–23 (NIV)

Recently, I had to drop my car off for service. Normally I get a ride back home or arrange a loan car, but this time I decided to take public transport. I discovered a bus route near the service facility that would take me home. Despite having driven down that road for decades, I could not remember ever seeing a bus stop. After dropping off my car, I walked down the road, somewhat sceptical about finding it. But to my surprise it was actually there, and the bus arrived on time and took me home.

On the ride, I reflected on how many times I had driven past that bus stop without noticing it. I had missed it because I was not looking for it. I wondered, *How often do I miss what God has done for me because I am not looking for it?* As a father, I know how it delights me when my children acknowledge something I have done on their behalf. Surely my heavenly Father is no different! I resolved to be more observant and consistent in praise to my heavenly Father. And I started with praising God for a safe trip home.

Prayer: *Dear Lord, thank you for the blessings you have provided. Help us to make praising you a daily habit. Amen.*

Thought for the day: For what will I praise God today?

Bill Gosling (Western Australia, Australia)

Enduring peace

Read Philippians 4:4–9

The peace of God, which surpasses all understanding, will guard your hearts and your minds in Christ Jesus.
Philippians 4:7 (NRSV)

Although at first glance it is not an attractive place to wander around or spend time in, Neath Abbey is a favourite quiet corner of mine. As soon as I step inside its grounds and stand on the grass, an awesome feeling of peace engulfs me.

Yet these ancient ruins have had some rough treatment down the years. As George Borrow noted, when he visited the site while trekking in Wales, its dilapidation was not due to time, but 'awful violence, possibly that of gunpowder'. He noted, too, that a tramway ran from the nearby ironworks into the abbey buildings; the walls are still blackened by massive scorch marks from long-gone smelting furnaces. Today, the ruins are surrounded by the mundane buildings of a business park and are often completely deserted, apart from an occasional dog walker.

I walk over to where the cloisters were and sit on the only bench in the whole place. Leaning back, I let the stillness seep into my whole being. *How can such a deeply spiritual peace*, I wonder, *have survived the industrial abuse which this sacred building has suffered?*

For me the answer is clear. Neath Abbey reminds me that, just as the apostle Paul wrote while in chains, the peace of God can endure through the most difficult of circumstances, guarding our hearts and minds as we come to God in prayer.

Prayer: *Dear Lord, may our hearts and minds be covered with your peace, even when we are surrounded by turmoil or busyness. Amen.*

Thought for the day: Regardless of my past or present circumstances, I can experience God's peaceful presence.

D. Carole Wilsher (Wales, United Kingdom)

Let God

Read Isaiah 55:6–13

In their hearts humans plan their course, but the Lord establishes their steps.
Proverbs 16:9 (NIV)

I was a Catholic seminarian for ten years. It had always been my dream to serve God and the church as a priest. However, after finishing my studies, I was not ordained. I was asked to take a leave of absence and explore life outside the seminary.

Upon hearing that I would not be ordained, waves of anger towards God came crashing over me, and I experienced a crisis of faith. I spent many sleepless nights thinking about my situation. I had done well in my studies; I prayed fervently and attended Mass piously. I thought I knew God to be gentle, loving and compassionate, and surely such a God would not take away my dream of becoming a priest.

When I sat down and re-evaluated myself, I realised that all along I had taken my eventual ordination for granted and had not let God be God in my life. I had grabbed the reins and taken control without truly asking God to guide me.

The past years have been a great blessing and an opportunity for me to know God more fully. I may not understand God's will, but I am now comforted by the truth that God is in charge of my life. I do not need to understand God's thoughts and ways to rely on God's will for me.

Prayer: *Lord God, we may not know what lies ahead for us, but we are assured of your promise that you will be with us every step of the journey. Amen.*

Thought for the day: I will release my control and trust in God.

Aldrin Nacu (Tarlac, Philippines)

Like a mother

Read Psalm 46:1–7

As a mother comforts her child, so I will comfort you; you shall be comforted in Jerusalem.
Isaiah 66:13 (NRSV)

My doctor told me that I needed a medical procedure. I dreaded having it, and as the day came closer I became more and more afraid. On the day of the procedure, I wore a T-shirt that had belonged to my mother. Feeling its soft material on my shoulders and arms, I remembered how my mother used to put her arms around me. When I was a small child and not feeling well, she would rock me and sing to me.

As the doctor gave me the anaesthesia, the memory of my mother comforting me reminded me that God also comforts us. I remembered scripture from the worship service that past Sunday: 'God is our refuge and strength, a very present help in trouble. Therefore we will not fear' (Psalm 46:1–2). I went to sleep feeling calm and peaceful as I once did in my mother's arms.

Prayer: *O God, help us to turn to you for comfort when we are afraid. We pray as Jesus taught us, 'Our Father in heaven, hallowed be your name, your kingdom come, your will be done, on earth as it is in heaven. Give us today our daily bread. And forgive us our debts, as we also have forgiven our debtors. And lead us not into temptation, but deliver us from the evil one' (Matthew 6:9–13, NIV). Amen.*

Thought for the day: God is like a mother comforting her child.

Cheryl Raley Wood (Tennessee, USA)

How does God see you?

Read 1 Peter 2:4–10

You are a chosen people, a royal priesthood, a holy nation, God's special possession, that you may declare the praises of him who called you out of darkness into his wonderful light.
1 Peter 2:9 (NIV)

I have struggled with speaking highly of myself. I always felt I was not good enough, even from a young age – not good enough to be successful, to fit in, to be appreciated, even to be loved. Most of these thoughts came from other people's opinions of me. But why do we think who we are depends on what others say about us?

Do we ever think about what God thinks of us? Do we believe in what God sees in us? God has already made it clear in scripture who we are. Today's quoted scripture reminds us that we are 'a chosen people'. It's up to us to believe and embrace that truth.

God chooses us out of unconditional love – not our social status or physical appearance. Understanding who we are in God's heart allows us to appreciate, accept and love ourselves, as well as those around us.

Prayer: *Dear God, help us always to know that our identity can be found in you. Remind us that we are your beloved and cherished people. Amen.*

Thought for the day: God's opinion of me is what matters most.

Hedina Ojwang (Nakuru County, Kenya)

Choosing to serve

Read 1 Corinthians 12:4–11

'Who is greater, the one who is at the table or the one who serves?
Is it not the one at the table? But I am among you as one who serves.'
Luke 22:27 (NRSV)

As I grew older, playing guitar, which had been my passion since the age of 13, fell by the wayside. When I was younger, I played in bands and would 'rock out' nearly every night. But I stopped having time for the hobby, and ultimately I lost touch with the instrument altogether.

A few years ago, when I was 61, a friend who played with our church's contemporary praise team approached me and asked if I would be interested in joining. I was nervous. Could I play anymore? If so, would I be good enough?

I took a chance and attended a rehearsal. I held back, lowered my volume and waited to see if I could add to the music. The group was welcoming, patient and kind. They supported me, and eventually I became a member.

I now have a better understanding of what Paul meant when he wrote, 'There are varieties of gifts but the same Spirit' (1 Corinthians 12:4). What we bring to the church is not as important as simply bringing something. God can speak through whatever we bring.

Prayer: *Dear God, thank you for the gifts you give to each of us and for the opportunity to serve alongside others. Amen.*

Thought for the day: How am I using my gifts to serve God?

David Balthrop (Kentucky, USA)

Fear not

Read Psalm 57:1–4

'I cry to God Most High, to God who fulfils his purpose for me.'
Psalm 57:2 (NRSV)

When I was 37 weeks pregnant with my only daughter, my doctor informed me that I would have to undergo a C-section. My oxygen levels had dropped, and my baby was having trouble breathing and was not moving as much as expected. I had an ultrasound and was then moved to the operating room for emergency surgery.

I was puzzled – and petrified. My husband was not with me, because I was with my parents. As I lay worried and afraid, my mother comforted me with these words: 'Fear not.' She reminded me that the Lord God was with me and would never leave me. She also told me of God's promise in Psalm 57:3 – that God who is faithful would surround me with love.

My mum's words gave me strength. By holding on to God's promise and blessings, I underwent my operation and received the biggest blessing of my life – my daughter. I will forever trust that no matter what the circumstance may be, my loving God is with me.

Prayer: *Dear God, thank you for the love and blessings which you bestow on us and our families. Give us strength to trust in your love for us when challenges arise. Amen.*

Thought for the day: God's blessings can come from the most difficult circumstances.

Rachana M. Ghazan (Uttar Pradesh, India)

Light for dark days

Read John 1:1–13
He said, 'I am the light of the world. Whoever follows me will never walk in darkness, but will have the light of life.'
John 8:12 (NIV)

A few years ago, my family and I witnessed a solar eclipse. The sky grew dark, the birds stopped chirping and the crickets came to life in the middle of the day. It was an eerie feeling. But it lasted only a few moments. If only other dark days could be so brief!

As the pastor of a church, I recently experienced a difficult situation with a church member. I felt discouraged and disillusioned hearing harsh words and criticisms.

While we can't remove the hurt any more than we can stop the moon from blocking the sun, we can remember the truths surrounding both. During a solar eclipse, we know that the sun is still shining; therefore, we wait in faith for its reappearance. When dark days come, we must remember that Christ still reigns, even if we can't see it. Therefore, we wait in faith for his reappearance.

But we don't wait idly. When darkness engulfs me, I turn to Jesus' words in scripture. As I meditate, Jesus becomes brighter and brighter in my soul. His presence fills me, and in his presence, darkness flees and light shines. Jesus is not just the light of the world; he's the light for our dark days.

Prayer: *Dear Father, help us to remember your promises when troubles and sorrows distract us from your presence. Amen.*

Thought for the day: I will embrace God's promises when difficult days come.

Eddie D. Fleming (Kentucky, USA)

Alone with God

Read Joshua 1:1–9
If God is for us, who can be against us?
Romans 8:31 (NIV)

When I was 18 years old, I moved across the world. I left my small home-town for the city of Sydney, Australia. As I stepped off the plane, I felt afraid. 'God, stay with me,' I prayed as I clenched my fists and looked up desperately to the sky. After a taxi ride that felt longer than it was, I set foot in my new home. The fear I had felt quickly turned into overbearing loneliness.

As I began to unpack, I pulled out my Bible. At the time, it seemed the only familiar sight in this strange, new country. Holding back tears, I decided to take a break from my unpacking and read God's word, thinking it might comfort me. I came upon the story of Joshua leading the Israelites into the promised land. Sydney, Australia, was as new and unknown to me as the promised land was to Joshua. But God frequently reminded Joshua and the Israelites not to be afraid.

Once I finished reading, I felt a great sense of comfort. The Lord spoke to me through Joshua's story, reminding me that I am never alone. Even when it seems that fear and loneliness are our only companions, God remains with us, holding us as we embark on any new adventure.

Prayer: *Ever-present God, help us remember that we are never alone because you are with us. Thank you for continuing to guide us each day. Amen.*

Thought for the day: Sometimes it takes being lonely to hear God's voice.

Kaitlyn Handy (Texas, USA)

Finding rest

Read Psalm 23

He makes me lie down in green pastures, he leads me beside quiet waters.
Psalm 23:2 (NIV)

I was designing a major installation at work. As the deadline approached, I began working overtime. It started as one extra hour a day but soon went to two hours a day overtime. The day before the deadline I worked from 7.00 am to 2.00 am the next morning. A few days later, my boss asked me to work away from home for six months. I had had enough, and I decided to resign. When my boss asked me why, I explained it to him. He gave me an extra week of annual leave and told me to rest!

Psalm 23 describes God as a shepherd who 'makes [us] lie down', giving us rest so that we can enjoy God's bountiful grace and mercy. God wants us to rest, to pause and focus on God. Even God paused to rest in the creation story (see Genesis 2:2–3).

We need physical rest, and we need emotional rest. Jesus said, 'Come to me, all you who are weary and burdened, and I will give you rest. Take my yoke upon you and learn from me, for I am gentle and humble in heart, and you will find rest for your souls. For my yoke is easy and my burden is light' (Matthew 11:28–30). God, through Jesus, offers rest for our souls.

Prayer: *Dear Jesus, help us to find rest in you. Show us how and when to rest. Amen.*

Thought for the day: Even when I am busy, I will follow God's example and pause to rest.

Robert Irvine (England, United Kingdom)

Hidden treasures

Read Matthew 6:19–21

We have this treasure in jars of clay to show that this all-surpassing power is from God and not from us.
2 Corinthians 4:7 (NIV)

When I was a child, my father and mother taught me the necessity of a daily connection with God. My father guided me by his example of living a godly life. My mother provided practical instruction by teaching my siblings and me how to pray, read the Bible and memorise scripture. Each morning before leaving for school, we learned those disciplines while gathered around the kitchen table. Mother always told us it was a great way to start the day and reminded us to live for Jesus as we rushed to catch our bus.

One of the verses I memorised around the kitchen table has become more significant to me as an adult: 'I treasure your word in my heart, so that I may not sin against you' (Psalm 119:11, NRSV). The Hebrew word for 'treasure' here can also be translated as 'store'. This means every verse of memorised scripture is stored in my heart, making them available to me even years later to draw upon in specific times of need.

Reading scripture draws us closer to God. When we treasure scripture in our hearts, we are 'prepared to do any good work' (2 Timothy 2:21), becoming living examples of faithfulness in the world.

Prayer: *Dear God, thank you for the gift of scripture. Help us to store your word in our hearts to strengthen us as we live for you. Amen.*

Thought for the day: How do I connect with God each day?

David J. Childress (Tennessee, USA)

Peace is ours

Read John 14:25–31

'Peace I leave with you; my peace I give you. I do not give to you as the world gives. Do not let your hearts be troubled and do not be afraid.'
John 14:27 (NIV)

When our oldest son was 18 months old, he started biting other kids. No matter what I said or did, he kept doing it. I stayed away from playgroups to avoid incidents, and I was anxious even when going out to lunch or visiting friends. I would cry at night feeling like I was being punished. I felt like this phase would never end, but eventually it did.

It's the same with life and what goes on in the world. When we dwell on current events, we lose our sense of peace and feel anxious. We forget that Jesus said, 'My peace I leave with you.' God doesn't wait for the storms to pass before giving us peace. Christ's peace is already here; it is ours.

The best way to keep the peace God has given us is to keep our eyes on God. How do we do that when we are bombarded with news of a world that seems to be breaking down? We read God's promises and spend time getting to know the Prince of Peace. We can only put out what we take in, so let's take God's word into our hearts.

Prayer: *Father God, help us when we let difficult situations interfere with the peace you have freely given. Allow the Prince of Peace to fill us with hope, faith and peace. In Jesus' name. Amen.*

Thought for the day: By spending time with God, I can turn my worries to peace.

Bongi Argyrou (Gauteng, South Africa)

Trusting God's will

Read Psalm 46:8–11

Jesus beheld them, and said unto them, With men this is impossible; but with God all things are possible.
Matthew 19:26 (KJV)

One rainy morning in July 2022, my nine-year-old son and I were getting ready for a very important visa appointment. We wanted to go to the country where my wife had been living for the past year. While travelling from our hotel to the embassy, my mind was racing. *What if we get the visas? What if we don't?* At the same time I was preparing myself to accept God's will.

During the interview with the visa officer, I discovered that I had all but one of our necessary documents with me. With prayers in my heart that a solution could be found, I said to the officer, 'I don't have that document with me today.' He assured me that he could help and searched for the document in his computer database. After some time, he printed that document for us. This was not a usual service offered by the visa office. If he had wished, the officer could have rejected our request.

This incident may sound mundane to many people, but I know in my heart that only God's power made that act of compassion possible. When we completely surrender ourselves to God's will, we open ourselves to experience God's wonderful deeds.

Prayer: *Father God, help us to understand that you are with us in all situations. Increase our faith, and help us to trust you fully. In Jesus' mighty name. Amen.*

Thought for the day: A small act of compassion can be the miracle I need.

Snehal Christian (Pennsylvania, USA)

A true relationship

Read Ephesians 1:3–14

'You will seek me and find me when you seek me with all your heart.'
Jeremiah 29:13 (NIV)

When I was growing up, my mother made sure that her four children were in church every Sunday. I was baptised and confirmed. In college, I met and later married a man who became a minister, and once again I was in church every week. I sang in the choir and served on committees. But it wasn't until I attended a spiritual retreat in my mid-30s that I realised that I had never actually developed a personal relationship with Jesus. I had been attending church all those years without really understanding just how Jesus was at work in my life.

During that retreat, I realised that I needed to make some changes. I wanted to get to know Jesus for myself, not just as someone else's good shepherd. Since then, I have made it my mission to develop a real relationship with Jesus and have come to know him better through Bible studies, devotional readings and active participation in worship. I have learned that we are each responsible for our own relationship with Jesus Christ.

Today, I am still in church just about every Sunday, but now it's not because of my mother or husband, although I am thankful for their influence. I'm there because I want to be. What a blessing this is!

Prayer: *Heavenly Father, thank you for the opportunities you give us to know you and your Son. Help us continue to grow in faithful obedience to you by following in the way Jesus taught. In his name we pray. Amen.*

Thought for the day: Attending worship is not a duty; it's a privilege.

Tricia Roe (Texas, USA)

Refreshed by God's creation

Read Genesis 1:1–13

God saw all that he had made, and it was very good.
Genesis 1:31 (NIV)

I enjoy walking in the park early in the morning. As I listen attentively to the singing of the birds, my soul offers praise to God with thanks for a new day. The beauty of creation reminds me that I, too, am God's precious creation, made to glorify my creator.

Sometimes it is hard to smile when storms upend our lives. In those times we can choose to spend our days in gloom and anger for the things we cannot bear, or we can soothe our spirits by spending time basking in God's creation. Those moments can then free us from the worries of today and fears of what tomorrow might bring.

In the face of uncertainty, surely our spirits will bloom again as we contemplate God's beautiful creation. If God cares about the birds of the air and the flowers in the field, God will certainly remember us too. When our souls are weary and in need of rest, we can sense God's presence through the works of God's hand and find our strength renewed.

Prayer: *Dear God, thank you for reminding us through your creation how much you love us. By admiring what your hands have made, help us to feel your presence each and every day. Amen.*

Thought for the day: I am God's precious creation.

Kumalawaty Sundari (Jakarta, Indonesia)

Filled with righteousness

Read Matthew 5:1–12

'Blessed are those who hunger and thirst for righteousness,
for they will be filled.'
Matthew 5:6 (NIV)

During a retreat, I was assigned to a table that included two residents of a substance-abuse treatment centre. I normally would have had no occasion to converse and pray with men in such circumstances, but God brought us together for a deep, spiritual experience. By the end of the retreat, I loved them like brothers.

The treatment centre is not far from my home, and I felt led to visit my new friends. They invited me to an evening worship service where I experienced a passion in worship that is hard to describe. I realised that these men are hungry for the word of God, they desperately want the Holy Spirit to transform them and they are not ashamed to say so. They have a lot to teach me.

From them, I learned I should not become complacent. Jesus said we will be filled with righteousness if we crave it like food and water, and I saw that intensity during the worship service. It caused me to ask myself, 'What am I hungry and thirsty for?' Jesus calls us to a righteousness that can only be obtained through him. I am thankful for the faith of my new friends and the lesson they have taught me.

Prayer: *Gracious God, we know that only you provide what truly nourishes us. Fill us with your love and grace until we are full. Amen.*

Thought for the day: When I seek Jesus, I will be filled.

Michael A. O'Quinn (Georgia, USA)

Unfamiliar paths

Read Psalm 25:1–15

Please lead me in your righteousness. Make your way clear, right in front of me.
Psalm 5:8 (CEB)

One morning I caught a ride before sunrise. As I rode in the back of the pickup truck, I could see hundreds of stars in the black sky, including familiar constellations. However, when I looked at the road ahead, illuminated by headlights, it didn't seem familiar at all. The barbed wire fence, trees and brush along the one-lane dirt road didn't look as I remembered. That surprised me since I have walked every inch of that mile-and-a-half stretch of road many, many times over the years. I was disoriented. Even so, I knew I would arrive at my destination soon.

As we continued, I thought about how sometimes life is like that. It can feel like we are travelling along unfamiliar paths. Yet signs of God's presence are all around us like shining stars if we only look – in scripture, in nature and in people. If we trust in God to guide us, we will receive just enough light to continue on until we reach our destination. We can trust that God will be with us as we journey and will lead us in the way we ought to go.

Prayer: *Dear Lord, help us to trust you to guide us. When our way seems unclear, turn us towards the signs of your presence. Amen.*

Thought for the day: Even when I don't know where I'm going, God does.

Sister Confianza del Señor (Colón, Honduras)

Dividing walls

Read Ephesians 2:11–22

He himself is our peace, who has made the two groups one and has destroyed the barrier, the dividing wall of hostility.
Ephesians 2:14 (NIV)

When my daughters were younger, they shared a bedroom. Most days, they viewed it as some sort of horrible punishment, and one day they'd had all they could take. When I walked into their room, I saw that they had placed a thick line of grey tape right down the middle of the room, leaving one half for each of them. The visual implication was clear: don't come across the line because what is over here belongs to me. I pulled up the tape dividing wall and reminded my daughters that they are part of one family – even in disagreements, we are still one.

The apostle Paul wrote to the church in Ephesus to remind them that Jews and Gentiles have been reconciled together through Jesus and that in Christ we are all one family: 'He himself is our peace, who has made the two groups one and has destroyed the barrier, the dividing wall of hostility.' Jesus did this through his death on the cross, bringing peace to humanity and reconciliation with God. As children of God, may we tear down the dividing walls of hostility and the barriers that are separating us today!

Prayer: *Gracious and loving God, thank you for removing the barriers that divide us from one another and separate us from you. Help us to live in harmony with one another through the peace that you have offered us in Jesus Christ, our Lord. Amen.*

Thought for the day: What barriers are dividing me from others and from God?

Michael Vaughn (Virginia, USA)

Get up!

Read Mark 2:1–12

He said to the man, 'I tell you, get up, take your mat and go home.'
Mark 2:11 (NIV)

'Ring!' goes the alarm. It is a sound most of us do not like much because it marks the time to leave a soft, warm bed to get up and start a new work day and take on daily responsibilities. And yet, we get up and begin the day.

The gospels offer several examples of how a command from Jesus is the impetus to go forward. To the paralyzed man who was carried by friends and lowered through the roof of a dwelling, Jesus said, 'Get up, take your mat and go home.' To the deceased young daughter of Jairus, the synagogue leader, Jesus said, 'My child, get up!' (Luke 8:54).

'Get up!' What an empowering statement from our Saviour to motivate us. Throughout the gospels, the Lord calls people to active service: 'Go… and preach' (Mark 16:15); 'Hand over your coat' (Matthew 5:40); 'Give to the one who asks you' (Matthew 5:42); 'Make disciples of all nations' (Matthew 28:19). However we serve, the Lord promises always to be by our side in our journey. All we have to do is follow Jesus' command and get up!

Prayer: *May your words continue to inspire us, O God, as we engage in active discipleship for the good of your kingdom. Amen.*

Thought for the day: I will serve the Lord with gladness.

Estela Baldeón (Lima, Perú)

My consolation

Read Psalm 34:15–18

My flesh and my heart may fail, but God is the strength of my heart and my portion forever.
Psalm 73:26 (NIV)

In 2009, my grandmother died of tuberculosis. I felt numb and weak with grief, but I couldn't cry until the burial day. I felt heavy watching the pallbearers lower her casket into the ground – I hated the idea of my grandmother being left all alone. I burst into uncontrollable tears and questioned God. But Tim, my older brother, gave me his shoulder to cry on. As if he knew my thoughts, he said, 'It's okay, she is with the Lord now – safe and happy.' I felt consoled that she wasn't alone.

Tim showed great consideration and selflessness by comforting me even though he was grieving too. Through Tim, God helped me to grieve. That experience reminds me that when I am feeling strong and emotionally stable, I have a responsibility to be considerate of those who may be more vulnerable or hurting.

God responded to my worry that day through Tim, whose words were exactly what I needed to hear. In that moment, I felt consoled, knowing that God had been with me all along.

Prayer: *Dear Lord, help us to be considerate of the needs of others. May we be their source of comfort and encouragement so that through us they can experience your unfailing grace. Amen.*

Thought for the day: Through me, God can offer strength and support to others.

Barnet Chokani Phiri (Nairobi, Kenya)

The eyes of the heart

Read John 9:35–41

I pray that the eyes of your heart may be enlightened.
Ephesians 1:18 (NIV)

I volunteer at a homeless shelter, and while I see many examples of kindness and support between guests using the service, at times I also witness disrespectful language and aggressive behaviour. Usually this is a result of drug and alcohol abuse or because of stronger personalities exploiting the more vulnerable. Seeing such behaviour can lead me to form judgements about the people involved.

However, listening to the personal stories of guests using the service, including neglectful or absent parents, limited access to education, life-long poverty, physical sickness, mental illness and frequent rejection, offers access into worlds I have no knowledge or experience of. Seeing with the eyes of the heart helps me to understand more about some of the challenges for those needing to use the shelter and why they might behave as they do.

In John 9, Jesus heals a man born blind. Physical sight is, indeed, a precious gift. But as Jesus points out to the Pharisees, one can see perfectly well, yet still be blind. Precious insights of life are revealed only when we look with the eyes of the heart. Jesus was criticised for spending much of his time in the company of 'sinners', but he looked at them with the eyes of his heart and was moved with compassion to heal, feed, nurture and finally to die for them.

Prayer: *Dear Lord Jesus, please open the eyes of our hearts that we might better understand what we observe. Amen.*

Thought for the day: 'People look at the outward appearance, but the Lord looks at the heart' (1 Samuel 16:7).

Jane Parker (England, United Kingdom)

God is working

Read Hebrews 11:1–10

Now faith is confidence in what we hope for and assurance about what we do not see.
Hebrews 11:1 (NIV)

I had registered for a professional examination that would be held outside of my town. I would need to travel, and the transportation fare was due one week before the examination day. Due to unforeseen circumstances, I had no money when it was time to pay the fare. However, I trusted that God would make a way for me, so I kept my faith alive. Surprisingly, just before the payment deadline, a friend called to check on me. She offered to cover all my expenses without asking for anything in return.

When we are close to giving up and feel like there is no way out of our situation, we do not need to despair. We don't need to know how God will work things out for us. We just need to keep our faith alive and trust that God is working and can bring about good things.

Prayer: *Dear God, when we don't see a way forward, strengthen our faith in you. Remind us of your goodness and provision as we pray the prayer Jesus taught us, 'Our Father which art in heaven, Hallowed be thy name. Thy kingdom come, Thy will be done in earth, as it is in heaven. Give us this day our daily bread. And forgive us our debts, as we forgive our debtors. And lead us not into temptation, but deliver us from evil: For thine is the kingdom, and the power, and the glory, forever. Amen' (Matthew 6:9–13, KJV).*

Thought for the day: God can see a way forward even when I cannot.

Deborah Oyelade (Oyo, Nigeria)

Letters from home

Read Matthew 18:10–14

'We had to celebrate and be glad, because this brother of yours was dead and is alive again; he was lost and is found.'
Luke 15:32 (NIV)

When our grandson was in high school he got into some trouble and was sent to a group home for teens. We earnestly desired to help him in any way we could, so we wrote him letters every day – notes on what we did that day, something inspirational, news about our church life and simply how we missed him.

After several months our family gathered to welcome our grandson home. He came around the corner with a big, appreciative smile while holding a pile of papers up to his chin. He had saved every letter we'd sent. He returned a changed and much more mature person.

We never know what will help others maintain their health and well-being and build their confidence. But communication is essential and good intentions show through. The letters we sent our grandson offered him solid support during trying times.

We don't always know the importance of our connections with others or how we can do the Lord's work even in small ways through them. But God is our fundamental sustainer, and Jesus is our ultimate inspiration and guide. Through prayer and helping others, we can give and receive comfort and solace.

Prayer: *Dear Lord, help us to notice those in need of connection. Guide us to do your work each day. Amen.*

Thought for the day: Openly communicating with others is one way I can do the Lord's work.

Bill Truran (New Jersey, USA)

Amazing grace

Read Daniel 3:24–30

We were buried with him by baptism into death, so that, just as Christ was raised from the dead by the glory of the Father, so we also might walk in newness of life.
Romans 6:4 (NRSV)

John Newton was born in London in 1725 to a Protestant mother and a father who was a ship captain. His mother died when he was almost seven years old, and as a boy he joined his father on his many voyages. John followed in his father's footsteps and became a ship captain, working in the transatlantic slave trade. During a voyage home, a horrendous storm blew in, putting the ship's crew and passengers in mortal danger. He prayed to God. The storm passed, and the ship was safe. John took this as a sign from God. It was a defining moment for him and inspired his faith. Gradually, he changed. He went on to become an ordained minister and abolitionist. He also wrote the words to the popular hymn 'Amazing Grace'. John Newton was transformed by his faith.

In the Bible, King Nebuchadnezzar experienced a similar transformation. It took the miracle of Shadrach, Meshach and Abednego surviving the furnace and his own wilderness experience (see Daniel 4:33–37) for Nebuchadnezzar to come to faith and truly believe in God.

Like John and Nebuchadnezzar, we too can be transformed. Through Christ, we are all made new. When we spend time in God's word and live in obedience to it, we can experience transformation.

Prayer: *Miraculous God, thank you for guiding us and turning us into something new. In Jesus' name. Amen.*

Thought for the day: God, through Jesus, makes all things new.

Velinda Scott (West Virginia, USA)

Who am I?

Read Exodus 3:1–12

Moses said to God, 'Who am I that I should go to Pharaoh and bring the Israelites out of Egypt?'
Exodus 3:11 (NRSV)

Moses is one of the most important figures in history. However, he spent most of his life in anonymity. After living the early part of his life among the Egyptian aristocracy, he became a shepherd and was quite old when God called him to a great mission.

God spoke to Moses through a magnificent revelation of power: a bush that burned with fire and was not consumed. However, Moses responded to God's call with a question: 'Who am I that I should go?' Moses' question makes sense. After all, he was a murderer and a fugitive (see Exodus 2:11–15). When Moses made excuses based on his incapacity, God refuted them saying, 'I will be with you.'

Many times in my life I have had to face circumstances that seemed beyond my capabilities. Better candidates always came to mind – people who could fulfil a divine mission more excellently. But the heavenly answer is always the same: 'I will be with you.' Then I understand: it is not about who I am but about the Holy One who calls me.

Prayer: *Dear God, thank you for being with us. Help us to trust you when you call us to do something we feel unprepared for. Amen.*

Thought for the day: When I feel unqualified, I will remember God's power.

Roberto Fernández-Acosta (Flanders, Belgium)

Hold my hand

Read Psalm 121

In my distress I cried unto the Lord, and he heard me.
Psalm 120:1 (KJV)

I was about to undergo a biopsy of the lump in my breast. After the nurse prepared me for the procedure, she left to get the doctor. Alone in the room, on the exam table, I whispered a short prayer: 'Jesus, hold my hand.' Moments later, the door opened and two nurses came in, followed by the doctor. The first nurse said, 'Hello, my name is "Hand Holder" because that is my job.' Her warm hand held mine as the biopsy was done.

Through the biopsy and the following cancer diagnosis and surgery, I put my trust in God, clinging tightly to the hand of Jesus. I cast all my cares on God because God cares for me (see 1 Peter 5:7). Jesus tells us not to worry. Our heavenly Father will take care of us. Jesus asks, 'Can any one of you by worrying add a single hour to your life?' (Matthew 6:27, NIV).

Jesus indeed held my hand during this difficult time in my life and gave me peace, assurance and hope. Isaiah 26:3 tells us that when we trust in and keep our thoughts on God, we can experience perfect peace. Now I am a five-year cancer survivor, filled with peace, hope and joy.

Prayer: *Dear Jesus, thank you for the peace of your presence, for hearing our prayers and for the comfort we find in you. Amen.*

Thought for the day: 'My soul clings to you; your right hand upholds me' (Psalm 63:8, NRSV).

Jeanne A. Everhart (Minnesota, USA)

An example to follow

Read Luke 6:32–36

'Love your neighbour as yourself.'
Matthew 22:39 (NIV)

As I drove towards the entrance to the industrial park where I work, there was heavy traffic on both sides of the street. I saw a woman in another car who wanted to make a U-turn, but no one on my side of the road was allowing her to turn. At the risk of frustrating the drivers behind me, I decided to let her make the turn and signalled for her to go ahead.

I watched her make the turn, feeling good about my kind action and expecting she would wave to express her thanks, but she didn't. My first thought was, *What an ungrateful person!* Then I paused to think more about what happened: *Why did I let the woman take the turn? What was my motive for that nice gesture towards a stranger?* Sadly, I had to admit that I had not acted out of generosity but rather to feel, if only briefly, the satisfaction of believing that I am a good person who did something good for someone. And, I was waiting for acknowledgment in return.

How easy it is to love when others reciprocate. But it is quite another matter when love or kindness is not reciprocated. Jesus is our ultimate example of selfless love – he gave his life for us. Today's scripture from Luke is a reminder and invitation to follow Jesus' example without waiting for anything in return.

Prayer: *Continue to inspire and prompt us, O Lord, to follow your example and live out your commandment to love one another, not because of anything we might receive in return but simply because you loved us first. Amen.*

Thought for the day: Wherever I am and in all that I do, I will follow the example of Jesus.

Roberto Rentería (Tamaulipas, México)

In the storm

Read Mark 4:35–41
A furious squall came up, and the waves broke over the boat, so that it was nearly swamped.
Mark 4:37 (NIV)

I sat alone at the kitchen table with an empty box of tissues. I'd been a Christian for years, but in that moment, my heart doubted what my head knew. If God loves me, why had this happened?

As I pondered my tempest, I remembered another storm – a ferocious one, 2,000 years ago on the Sea of Galilee. I realised that this story isn't just about a storm but also a journey of trust. The disciples followed Jesus, but the storm still came. They shouted at Jesus, asking him the same question I often do: 'Lord, don't you care?'

Storms may cause us to question God's care for us. We pray for healing, protection and restoration – for the storm to pass. It's not wrong to pray for that. But we must learn to value God's presence in our trials more than we value respite from them.

Jesus calmed the storm on the Sea of Galilee. Sometimes he doesn't calm our storms, but he guides us through them. When doubts arise, we can remember that Jesus is with us in the storm.

Prayer: *Dear Jesus, help us to trust you, especially during trials. Help us to remember you are always with us, no matter what we face. Amen.*

Thought for the day: Life's storms can bring me closer to Jesus.

Glenda Durano (New Mexico, USA)

Our great provider

Read Psalm 146

My God will meet your every need out of his riches in the glory that is found in Christ Jesus.
Philippians 4:19 (CEB)

My mother died when I was very young. Her death was so sudden that my family and I could not understand what had happened or why. My father was a clergyman and had served the Lord in church all his life, but I felt that my mother's devotion and prayers kept my family together and happy. She used to get up early and wake us up for morning devotions. We used to sing hymns, pray and read the Bible together as a family. When my mother died, I wondered how we would survive without her.

However, we continued the habit of praying every morning. We prayed for peace and comfort in our family. And our friends and relatives prayed for us too. I was surprised that I could actually feel God's comfort in my heart. I could feel that people were praying for us.

This experience taught me that when we need comfort, God will provide it. God is indeed a great provider who knows our needs.

Prayer: *Dear God, thank you for your providence. Comfort us when we grieve, and guide us to pray for and help those in need of comfort. Amen.*

Thought for the day: What faith practices sustain me in challenging times?

Ruth Haroon (Punjab, Pakistan)

Who is my neighbour?

Read Mark 3:31–35

'Whoever does the will of God is my brother and sister and mother.'
Mark 3:35 (NRSV)

As a child I was confused about who I could be friends with. My next door neighbours on either side of our terraced house were not of the same denomination as our family, so I was encouraged to avoid them. They looked normal and friendly, and I could not understand why my mother was unreceptive towards them.

One day while I was playing in our enclosed backyard, I could see the top of the head of the girl next door over the wall. We started talking, and she invited me to come over and play with her. I opened the gate between our properties and went to play with her, and this was the beginning of a lasting friendship.

For me it was also the beginning of my ecumenical journey. As I grew into adulthood I came to understand that all who recognise Jesus as God's Son are part of his family. The church has a sad history of sectarian conflict, and there is much division still (though thankfully less violent than in the past). But we are all made in the image of God and each have a role to play in the building up of God's kingdom here on earth. Jesus stated as much when he declared: 'Whoever does the will of God is my brother and sister and mother.'

Prayer: *Help us, Father God, to love our neighbours as ourselves, especially our brothers and sisters in Christ. Amen.*

Thought for the day: With God, there are no favourites (see Galatians 2:6).

Betty Madill (Scotland, United Kingdom)

No fear in love

Read 1 John 4:13–18

There is no fear in love. But perfect love drives out fear, because fear has to do with punishment. The one who fears is not made perfect in love.

1 John 4:18 (NIV)

I served as a pastor in the village of Donetsk, Ukraine. Our street was at the edge of the village, and we could see the front line of the war from our window. Opposing troops were stationed nearby – just over 300 yards away. A woman who lived on our street used to visit our church, but things changed when the war started in 2014. The village was heavily shelled, and people were terrified. This woman was shocked by the explosions and was afraid of every loud noise, even a knock on the gate. She crawled under the table and refused to come out.

Neighbours managed to get her to go with them to our church meeting. We prayed for her and told her about the love of God. It wasn't long before she started to smile. A great change took place in her life. She told us, 'Now I have peace in my heart because I know that God loves me. During bombings I can praise my God. I can even sleep peacefully at night.' No matter our circumstances, we can trust in God's promise to watch over us, and we can experience true peace through Jesus Christ.

Prayer: *Heavenly Father, help us to find peace, even in terrifying situations, and to experience your love. Amen.*

Thought for the day: In every situation, God's love will sustain me.

Halyna Kovalenko (Ukraine)

PRAYER FOCUS: PEOPLE LIVING IN WAR ZONES

Living with purpose

Read Philippians 1:22–26

Whatever you do, whether in word or deed, do it all in the name of the Lord Jesus, giving thanks to God the Father through him.
Colossians 3:17 (NIV)

As someone who has been happily retired for the past ten years, I am occasionally asked for advice by friends who are approaching retirement. If I had to boil it down to one main point, my advice would be: 'Live with purpose.'

The life of the apostle Paul gives us a wonderful example. After encountering the resurrected Christ on the Damascus Road, Paul spent the remainder of his life proclaiming the good news of the gospel everywhere he travelled. Despite being beaten, stoned, shipwrecked and imprisoned, Paul kept his focus on preaching Christ. He summed up his purpose by writing, 'To me, to live is Christ and to die is gain' (Philippians 1:21).

Retirement usually provides more free time, so it's important to reflect on our priorities and then use the extra time wisely. But that guidance isn't just for retirement; our goal should be to live with purpose no matter how old we are or in what stage of life we find ourselves. As followers of Jesus, our purpose should be focused on living for him. Again, Paul sums it up well: '[Christ] died for all, that those who live should no longer live for themselves but for him who died for them and was raised again' (2 Corinthians 5:15).

Prayer: *Heavenly Father, guide us so that we keep our focus on living for you – through witness, service and worship. May we bring glory to your name by living as courageous Christ-followers. Amen.*

Thought for the day: I live with purpose when I follow the way of Jesus.

John D. Bown (Minnesota, USA)

Constant motion

Read 1 Kings 19:11–15

'The wind blows wherever it pleases. You hear its sound, but you cannot tell where it comes from or where it is going. So it is with everyone born of the Spirit.'
John 3:8 (NIV)

As I sit on the patio, the breeze brushes against my face and I can feel the wind and hear it as it swirls through the trees. I have learned to see and enjoy God in everything. Like a gentle breeze, God's presence is all around. God fills the space around us and is in constant motion – always working, always breathing life into us.

Scripture tells us in 1 Kings 19 that Elijah was disturbed and confused after a spiritual battle that sapped his strength. As he stood at the mouth of the cave where he had taken refuge, God was in a gentle whisper that gave Elijah new strength and direction that his life needed. No matter what life brings, we can be certain that God is in constant motion, filling the space around us, as the impulse of the Holy Spirit inspires and guides us.

Prayer: *Spirit of the Living God, teach us to recognise signs of your presence all around us. Even when we do not know the direction the Holy Spirit is taking, inspire us to believe and follow where you lead. Amen.*

Thought for the day: Today I will pay attention to how the Holy Spirit is moving in and around me.

Norma Gabriela Stieben (Entre Ríos, Argentina)

My dream job

Read Proverbs 3:5–8

In all your ways acknowledge [the Lord], and he will make straight your paths.
Proverbs 3:6 (NRSV)

A family member once asked me to describe my dream job. I was a sixth-grade teacher at the time, but my honest answer was to become a mother. I now have that job, but there are moments when it doesn't feel like the dream. When family members are tired and cranky, when loads of laundry pile up and multiple errands must be run, it becomes easy to lose sight of the blessings.

During these times, I must acknowledge God's presence in my life, refocus and remind myself how truly blessed I am – doing just what my heart desired. It is a privilege to take care of those I love day by day.

Therefore, when our sink is filled with dishes and laundry baskets are full, I am thankful for food to eat and clothes to wear. When my house needs a thorough cleaning, I am grateful for the lives that move within it each day. As I clean up after pets or pull weeds in the garden, I become aware of the beauty of God's creation. When I am completely exhausted, what a blessing it is to end a long day by snuggling my sweet son as he falls asleep and talking with my husband in the quiet of the evening! In the midst of life's busyness and day-to-day tasks, let's remember God's many gifts to us.

Prayer: *Dear God, when we feel worn down, help us to be grateful and to see each task we do as a gift from you. Amen.*

Thought for the day: In difficult moments, I will give thanks for God's blessings.

Sheryl Black Chai (Tennessee, USA)

Weaving a new life

Read 1 John 1:5–10

If we confess our sins, he is faithful and just and will forgive us our sins and purify us from all unrighteousness.
1 John 1:9 (NIV)

One day several years ago, I was weaving an obi on my home loom. The obi (the wide sash of a Japanese kimono) had been designed by an acquaintance. While studying the pattern of the complex combination of various colours, I proceeded cautiously.

However, one morning I discovered a mistake in the portion I had been weaving the previous day. I had proceeded quite a ways from that point. Frustrated, I prayed to the Lord and slowly began the process of untying the necessary threads while being very careful not to damage those that could remain. I worked the entire day and finally got back to the place that needed to be redone. Then, using the correct thread, I was able to weave the obi in accordance with the design as though I had never made the mistake.

Later, I thought of the death and resurrection of Jesus for our seemingly irreversible sin, a sacrifice that makes us new – as though we had never sinned! In the course of our life, there are times when we make choices that alter the direction of our lives. But when we repent and receive God's forgiveness, we can follow the pattern that God designed for us.

Prayer: *Our Father in heaven, thank you for forgiving our sins. As we repent, help us to become more holy – more like Christ. Amen.*

Thought for the day: No matter my mistakes, Jesus offers me forgiveness.

Akemi Kawashima (Saitama, Japan)

Beauty from brokenness

Read John 10:7–15

The thief comes only to steal and kill and destroy; I have come that they may have life, and have it to the full.
John 10:10 (NIV)

It arrived in the post, totally unexpected – the most beautiful mosaic panel. A floral design in glorious purple and turquoise with flashes of red and green on a pearl background sparkled like stained-glass windows or expensive jewellery. But there was nothing expensive about this. Closer inspection showed plaster embedded with beads from broken necklaces and shards of old glass and pottery, skilfully blended into a satisfying whole – a work of art; a thing of great beauty.

And it was made with love, not by a professional artist but by a friend who had picked up mosaic-making to help him in his role as long-term carer for his severely disabled wife. Theirs has been a life of struggles and disappointments but, radiating from their faith, one of joy and triumph too. That panel mirrored their life.

John 10:10 has been my favourite Bible verse since I first became a Christian many years ago. But it took that mosaic to demonstrate to me the true meaning of life 'to the full'. A full life here on earth comprises not only contentment and good times, but sorrow, hardship and brokenness too. Indeed, they are a necessary part of the truly full life.

Prayer: *Dear Lord, we thank you for opening the way to life in all its fullness. Strengthen our faith when we struggle and teach us to trust you through all life's challenges. Amen.*

Thought for the day: With God there is no experience that cannot be transformed and used for good.

Alison Cross (England, United Kingdom)

Refusing to participate

Read Romans 12:17–21

'You have heard that it was said, "An eye for an eye and a tooth for a tooth." But I say to you: Do not resist an evildoer. But if anyone strikes you on the right cheek, turn the other also.'
Matthew 5:38–39 (NRSV)

This year I participated in a defensive driving course designed to teach students to be more thoughtful and careful drivers. The class covered several subjects, among them road rage. 'What do you do,' the instructor addressed me, 'when faced with an instance of road rage?'

I reflected on the many times drivers had honked the horn to urge me to speed, cut me off or tailgated my vehicle. 'Nothing,' I replied. 'I just keep going my own way.'

'That', he said, 'is the correct answer. Do not fuel the other driver's anger with your reaction. It serves no positive purpose. Just go your own way.'

I thought about how this has been my policy in other aspects of my life as well. Fuelling the flame of another's anger serves no positive purpose. In the gospel of Matthew, Jesus admonishes us to turn the other cheek towards those who do us harm. With that in mind, I've found that a smile, a friendly nod, a compliment, a joke or simply not reacting can quickly disarm a tense situation. What other creative ways could we find to turn the other cheek?

Prayer: *Parent of us all, help us to be calm examples of your goodness, patience and mercy in all situations. Amen.*

Thought for the day: Anger is disarmed when I refuse to participate.

Monica A. Andermann (New York, USA)

Light of hope

Read Jonah 2:1–10

From inside the fish Jonah prayed to the Lord his God. He said:
'In my distress I called to the Lord, and he answered me.'
Jonah 2:1–2 (NIV)

For several days now I have been feeling depressed – as if life is weighing me down, as if I can't breathe fresh air, as if I were at the bottom of the sea. Outwardly, I am all smiles, but inside I feel a knot in my chest. Still, deep within me I trust in God and God's plan. Though today it seems like I have run into a dead end, God's purpose will be fulfilled.

I believe it is important to share and speak of the difficult moments we endure as well as the joy of the miracles we receive. Every new morning signals an invitation for us to be grateful for at least one thing, to trust in God's promises and not to lose heart. After all, God protected Daniel in the lions' den (see Daniel 6:23), watched over Joseph when his brothers threw him into a well (see Genesis 37), and brought Jonah out of the great fish (see Jonah 2:10). Dark moments and distress will continue to test our faith, but we will be victorious when we remain anchored in our faith and seek God's light of hope.

Prayer: *Light of the world, guide us with love through each day.*
As you help us move forward, we pray with confidence and renewed hope the prayer Jesus taught us: 'Father, hallowed be your name, your kingdom come. Give us each day our daily bread. Forgive us our sins, for we also forgive everyone who sins against us. And lead us not into temptation' (Luke 11:2–4). Amen.

Thought for the day: God's light will shine through any darkness.

María de los Ángeles Vélez (Santiago, Chile)

Second chances

Read Luke 15:11–24

Peter came to Jesus and asked, 'Lord, how many times shall I forgive my brother or sister who sins against me? Up to seven times?' Jesus answered, 'I tell you, not seven times, but seventy-seven times.'
Matthew 18:21–22 (NIV)

I grew up with three brothers. As rambunctious boys, our childish antics often tested the patience of our loving parents. On occasion, one of us would do something that required correction from our parents. My childish apologies were usually sincere. Sometimes there were tears involved, but my parents made it clear that I was loved and forgiven. It was almost as if the infraction had never happened.

The Bible contains many stories of repentance and forgiveness, but perhaps the story of forgiveness that is most clear to me is the parable of the prodigal son. The young man demanded his inheritance, left home for a life of sinfulness, lost everything, and then came back home in shame. He didn't deserve forgiveness, but his father welcomed him back with open arms.

We all make mistakes, but there is power in forgiveness. When we forgive, we are freed from bitterness and anger; when we are forgiven, we are freed from guilt and shame. Forgiveness brings us into a closer relationship with God the Father. When we come to God in repentance and ask for another chance, God always forgives us.

Prayer: *Merciful God, thank you for forgiving us again and again. Help us to learn from your example so that we can more readily forgive others. In Jesus' name we pray. Amen.*

Thought for the day: God offers me a life of second chances.

Doug Wingert (Arizona, USA)

I AM

Read Psalm 104:10–13

God said to Moses, 'I AM WHO I AM. This is what you are to say to the Israelites: "I AM has sent me to you."'
Exodus 3:14 (NIV)

One day I decided to change the background images on my desktop computer. While I explored the possibilities, I found a series of photographs, each featuring a path winding through woods, climbing high mountain passes or twisting through dunes towards the seashore. Each photograph seemed to explore a facet of creation – each a beautiful moment captured in time. Like Moses in front of the burning bush in Exodus 3, I stopped and marvelled at each scene.

Too often on our life journeys, we become preoccupied by negative past experiences or anxious visions of the future and don't appreciate the beauty of the present. In doing so, we miss much. God is not simply I was or I will be but I AM.

There is more richness around us than we realise. Perhaps we will catch the song of a blackbird, the glow of a fiery sunset, the movements of a caterpillar or the aroma of fresh bread. And as we do, we may also glimpse something of God: creativity, majesty, goodness, even humour. God knows our struggles but has a plan for us and promises to be with us. Even now, God may be calling us towards new challenges and a chance to make a difference.

Prayer: *Father God, give us eyes to see the wonders around us and the courage to respond when you reveal yourself. Amen.*

Thought for the day: When I pause to notice the beauty around me, I catch glimpses of God.

April McIntyre (England, United Kingdom)

Joyful service

Read John 13:1–17

'Since you know these things, you will be happy if you do them.'
John 13:17 (CEB)

On the first morning of our cruise, my wife and I were eating breakfast in the cafe. We overheard a conversation between a busboy and the people seated at a nearby table. It soon became apparent from their dialogue that the man clearing the table was not a busboy but the ship's captain! Despite his important position on the ship, he occasionally waits on tables, allowing him to engage with all the passengers on the voyage.

In today's familiar passage from the gospel of John, Jesus washes his disciples' feet to teach an important lesson: if he, our Lord, is willing to serve others, we need to be willing to do the same. He said, 'I have given you an example.' He then added that happiness comes from following his example. Jesus' teaching contradicts society's norm by telling us that happiness comes from serving others, not from others serving us. There is a special joy that accompanies serving others in a spirit of humility. It is not enough simply to agree with Christ's teaching; we must also follow his example.

Prayer: *Loving Lord, help us to follow the way of life you lived on earth. Show us whom we can serve today, and give us the humility to do so. Amen.*

Thought for the day: I will find happiness when I serve others.

Wayne Greenawalt (Wisconsin, USA)

The vineyard

Read Matthew 20:1–16

'Am I not allowed to do what I choose with what belongs to me? Or are you envious because I am generous?'
Matthew 20:15 (NRSV)

There was a major project at work. A co-worker I had never met was assigned to help me, but she was not there yet. The day went on, and I did the job alone. When she finally arrived, there were only two hours left in the workday. I was angry that I had already completed most of the work. Instead of working with her, I went on my own to finish the part of the project that I had started.

Then I recalled Jesus' parable about the workers in the vineyard. Some people went to work later in the day in that story too, but the landowner showed all the workers the same respect, giving them equal pay. Like some of the workers in the parable, I had expected more for my hard day's work – perhaps not more pay but at least more appreciation.

I was only human, and my feelings were normal. As I acknowledged my own feelings and thought about the parable, I began to understand Jesus' teaching more fully. Jesus' parable encourages us to show compassion rather than anger because God loves us all. When our workday was done, I thanked my co-worker for the contributions she had made to the project that afternoon.

Prayer: *Dear God, thank you for Jesus' teachings in scripture. Help us to reflect on his words and apply them to our daily lives. In his name we pray. Amen.*

Thought for the day: I will follow Jesus' teachings and show compassion to those around me.

Sonya Monts (North Carolina, USA)

Even the unprepared

Read 1 Samuel 16:1–13

'You didn't choose me, but I chose you and appointed you so that you could go and produce fruit and so that your fruit could last.'
John 15:16 (CEB)

When I first gave my life to Christ, I was heavily involved with church activities – I wanted to know more of God. Less than a year later, my church's youth president left unexpectedly, and the position became vacant. One Sunday, the provincial pastor showed up unannounced and said he would appoint a church member as the youth president that day. Ultimately, I was chosen. But I had not received religious education or training. I was simply a zealous member who was always present at church events. But once I was appointed, I started training for the role. In a short time, to the glory of God, I had built a youth community that had never existed before in the church.

Studying scripture over the years, I have realised that God often uses people who are unprepared or unqualified. Gideon felt unqualified in his own eyes (see Judges 6:11–16). David's family least expected him to be chosen by God (see 1 Samuel 16:6–13). The apostle Paul was against Christ (see Acts 9:1–16).

God can use anyone. No matter our past or our abilities, when we surrender ourselves totally, God will empower us for the work we are called to do.

Prayer: *Heavenly Father, use us as your vessels to spread the gospel and build your kingdom in Jesus' name. Amen.*

Thought for the day: God will use me for a good purpose.

Adefioye Adebayo Benjamin (Lagos, Nigeria)

Use me to serve

Read Psalm 37:3–6

Take delight in the Lord, and he will give you the desires of your heart.
Psalm 37:4 (NIV)

I retired from teaching after more than 30 years, leaving a profession I loved. I wondered how I would fill my days, which had once been busy with lesson planning, correcting papers and school activities. I prayed to God: *Please use me to serve, Lord*.

A few days later, I received a visit from a minister in our community. She explained that a local food outreach had closed. With all the food insecurity and poverty in our county and surrounding areas, this outreach was very much needed. The ministerial association had come up with a new idea for outreach – a mobile food pantry. I was asked to be a part of this ministry that would help bridge the hunger gap for those in rural areas. A month later, we held our first event and distributed free baskets of food.

The mobile food pantry, comprised entirely of volunteers, is now in its eleventh year, and I continue to serve as the chair. God truly does give us the desires of our heart when we delight in God.

Prayer: *Thank you, Lord, for how you care for each of us. We are grateful for people and ministries that help feed those who are hungry. Amen.*

Thought for the day: Today I will look for opportunities to serve God and those around me.

Kris Gunderson (Iowa, USA)

Street of joy

Read Isaiah 43:9–13

'You are my witnesses,' declares the Lord, 'that I am God.'
Isaiah 43:12 (NIV)

I grew up in a small town in South India, in a neighbourhood called Ananda Peta, which means 'street of joy'. It truly was a place of joy for me and my siblings, as well as many cousins and friends. Every evening we would gather on the street to play games. Our church, built by my grandfather, was central to our close-knit community.

This neighbourhood of joy shaped my faith in Christ and nurtured me into the person I have become – a teacher, a minister and an advocate for women. Many of the children I grew up with went on to become doctors, nurses, teachers, pastors and government officials. Some of them became missionaries, providing healthcare and education.

In Acts 1:8 Jesus told his disciples, 'You will receive power when the Holy Spirit comes on you; and you will be my witnesses… to the ends of the earth.' I believe we kids did receive the Holy Spirit's power, and we dispersed into the world to become witnesses of the love and joy we have in Christ. May we never underestimate the lasting impact of childhood experiences of joyful play, community celebrations and shared Bible stories.

Prayer: *Living God, help us to be your witnesses, filled with your Spirit. We need your unfailing grace and abiding presence in our lives. In Christ's name. Amen.*

Thought for the day: Faith grows through both play and worship.

Navamani Peter (Karnataka, India)

Why are you here?

Read 1 Kings 19:1–9

He came to a broom bush, sat down under it and prayed that he might die. 'I have had enough, Lord,' he said.
1 Kings 19:4 (NIV)

Elijah had humiliated King Ahab and Queen Jezebel. Terrified for his life because of Jezebel's vow to exact revenge, Elijah fled. In his exhaustion, he uttered a phrase my heart has felt many times: 'I have had enough, Lord!' I can imagine the relief welling up in the prophet's heart as he entered into the safety of God's mountain after his long, arduous journey. But before Elijah could catch his breath or gather his thoughts, God asked, 'Why are you here?' On one level the question implied that Elijah should be elsewhere, completing the work the Lord had given him to do. On another level, it prompted him to consider his heart's motivation.

Like Elijah, I sometimes find myself crying out, 'I've had enough!' while facing resistance in ministry. Unconstructive criticism on how I teach Sunday school or lead music wears me down. Parents disrupting the teen ministry frustrates me. Volunteers failing to follow through is discouraging. In these moments I, too, have to answer God's question, *Why are you here?* I ask myself, *Why am I really doing what I'm doing?*

Reminded of God's holiness, Elijah was refreshed and went on to fulfil an extraordinary destiny. When we pause to evaluate our motivations and realign them with God's will, we can find renewed zeal in our service to God and others.

Prayer: *Dear Lord, help us align our motivations with yours so that we can be refreshed and strengthened as we work with you. Amen.*

Thought for the day: What is my motivation for serving God?

Megan L. Anderson (Indiana, USA)

God cares for us

Read Psalm 145:14–21

'Look at the birds of the air; they do not sow or reap or store away in barns, and yet your heavenly Father feeds them. Are you not much more valuable than they?'
Matthew 6:26 (NIV)

When I found out my wife was pregnant, I was thrilled. Then we learned she was pregnant with twins, and I was worried we would not be able to meet all their needs. After eight months, Jedidiah and Noah were born.

The first two years were the hardest because our sons were born prematurely and needed extra attention. My wife resigned from her job so she could devote herself fully to caring for the twins. As new parents, we faced many struggles, especially financially since my wife's income used to support our family. We needed so much money for milk, food and clothes, and I felt desperate to fulfil all the needs. Pondering Jesus' words that our Father feeds even the birds of the air strengthened me during that period.

God miraculously met all our needs. On numerous occasions, the Lord has demonstrated great care for us by providing us with necessities such as milk, diapers and clothing. The Lord has used good friends and sometimes strangers to support our needs. Truly God cares for us much more than for the birds of the air!

Prayer: *Dear God, thank you for the comfort you offer us in scripture. Help us remember that you will provide for us in our times of need. Amen.*

Thought for the day: How can I be an instrument of God's miraculous provision?

Ayub Simanjuntak (West Java, Indonesia)

Like trees walking around

Read Mark 8:22–26
Then his eyes were opened, his sight was restored, and he saw everything clearly.
Mark 8:25 (NIV)

For playground ball games in primary school, I was always the last one chosen for a team. No one wanted me because I could never accurately hit or catch a ball. I was hurt by the rejection, but I was even more frustrated by my own clumsiness.

When I was a young adult, I found out that I needed glasses with prism lenses to correct my double vision. Without them, I had no depth perception. No wonder I struggled at ball games as a child! If my classmates had known about my vision problem, maybe they would have been more merciful. If I had known about it, I could have been more merciful towards myself.

Just as my classmates complained about me, I often criticise people – silently or even out loud – for their mystifying behaviour: *How can they act so foolishly? Don't they see how they make trouble for themselves and everybody else?* Then sometimes I discover what's really going on in their lives. They may be going through a crisis at home, or maybe they've suffered a great personal loss.

Like the man in today's scripture reading, I have not seen these people clearly but like 'trees walking around' (Mark 8:24). I need Jesus' help to see them fully – as real people who face real difficulties.

Prayer: *Dear Lord, help me to see other people as you see them. Amen.*

Thought for the day: Today I will look at people with compassion rather than judgement.

Sandy Larsen (Minnesota, USA)

Songs of praise

Read Psalm 100

Worship the Lord with gladness; come before him with joyful songs.
Psalm 100:2 (NIV)

While standing at the bus stop recently, I heard the melodious singing of an Australian magpie. Looking around, I spotted the bird perched on the roof of a nearby house. With his beak raised skyward and head thrown back, he was filling the air with song in wonderful, happy abandonment, praising his maker with his whole being.

It came to me that he was a role model for how we should praise God, and I wished I were as uninhibited in my praise as the magpie! For me, playing and singing hymns is one of the ways I feel moved to praise God. The music is powerfully uplifting, and the words of the hymns remind me how faithful and loving God is and the grace God has given us through Jesus Christ. Praising God with music lifts my spirit and causes me to remember God's blessings. Then I am left with a thankful heart, which can brighten even the greyest of days.

Prayer: *Loving God, thank you for the gifts of music and song. We praise you for your goodness, love and care for us. May our hearts never cease to praise you. Through Jesus Christ, we pray. Amen.*

Thought for the day: Today I will praise God without inhibitions.

Margaret Martin (Australian Capital Territory, Australia)

Enduring adversity

Read Matthew 6:25–34

*Do not fear, for I am with you; do not be dismayed, for I am your God.
I will strengthen you and help you; I will uphold you with my righteous
right hand.*
Isaiah 41:10 (NIV)

At a young age, I faced the heartbreaking loss of my father and grew up
separated from my mother due to our impoverished background. Life
became even more difficult when I tragically lost my mother when I was
17. I endured threats and physical abuse as I pursued my education. In
search of peace, I made the difficult decision to flee my country.

Throughout my journey, my faith in God has not wavered as I have
witnessed God's hand at work, giving me the strength to persevere. God
blessed me with a resilient and positive mindset, which has sustained me.

Matthew 6:26 reminds us of God's unwavering love and care for us,
which assures us that we are valuable. This encourages me to trust in
God's providence during challenging times. Isaiah 41:10 reminds us that
God is always by our side, ready to offer strength, help and support. With
God as my constant companion, I know I can face any challenge.

Though my journey to find peace is ongoing, I find solace knowing God
remains faithful. I choose to focus on the positive aspects of my story,
for they remind me of the resilience and faith that have carried me this
far. I am confident that as I continue to rely on God's strength, I will find
the peace and fulfilment I am searching for.

Prayer: *Dear God, we seek your grace and guidance. Guide our steps
and fill our hearts with your love. Amen.*

Thought for the day: With God's help, I can face life's challenges with
unwavering faith.

Clovis Nkemzemoh (New Jersey, USA)

The practice of hope

At the beginning of Advent my five-year-old asked me, 'How old is Jesus?' I paused, not knowing exactly how to answer the question. 'What do you mean?' I asked. 'Jesus was a baby last Christmas, so how old is he now?'

I don't remember exactly how I answered the question, but we had a good conversation about celebrating Christmas and Jesus' continual presence with us. My daughter's question, however, illuminated for me how confusing the liturgical calendar can be. Each year we celebrate the birth of Jesus and the coming of Christ's light into the world. Then through Holy Week we follow the life and ministry of Christ and the despair of death before rejoicing at the miracle of Christ's resurrection. This cycle of hope and desolation is built into the rhythm of our Christian faith, and we repeat it year after year.

Amid Christmas celebrations, hope might be easier to see and hold on to. But as the Christmas season ends and we march through Epiphany and towards the early ministry of Jesus, the wilderness experience and Lent loom before us. Hope starts to feel more distant. How do we hold on to hope knowing that wilderness and death lie ahead?

In popular culture, we often talk about hope as something dictated by our circumstances and easily lost depending on the situation. Such an idea has recently felt particularly challenging and unhelpful to me. News accounts are filled with war and violence, fear and discord, hunger and suffering. Where do we find hope when world events seem far from hopeful? Our Christian faith and the cycle of the liturgical calendar offer an answer: instead of a possession, hope is an action – something we practise even when we don't feel all that hopeful.

Ritual is one way we practise hope. Jesus gave us two specific models for what the practice of hope through ritual might look like. In the Lord's Prayer, he gave us words to say, a vision for what is possible with God's help, and ways for us to participate with God in the world. When we pray the words Jesus taught us, we practise hope. We remind ourselves of

God's power and mercy, and we hold ourselves accountable for reflecting that mercy to others. We recognise that we are not perfect – that life is not perfect – but as we pray the words, we acknowledge the belief and trust that with God the world can be better. And what is that if not hope?

Likewise, the Lord's supper gives us actions to perform and words to recall that sustain us until Christ comes again. Recalling and naming Christ's divine power over death is perhaps the greatest act of hope we can engage in. When we pray, participate in the Lord's supper, attend worship or read scripture, we are acting on what we believe to be possible and true, even when it doesn't feel fully present or 'real'.

Parenting circles these days are fond of rewriting the old adage 'Practice makes perfect' to 'Practice makes better.' I think this is especially true of the practice of hope. After all, we will never hope perfectly – that is to say, without doubt or fear. But practicing hope makes us more attuned to God at work in the world, better able to see possibility instead of bleakness and more prepared to act for justice and with compassion when the world's strife begins to overwhelm us.

Now more than ever we need to practise hope through prayer, ritual, compassion and curiosity. Practising hope sustains us in the wilderness until we can celebrate the Easter promise of resurrection and the rebirth of hope in the person of the Christ child.

As this new year begins, how can you plan to practise hope?

QUESTIONS FOR REFLECTION

1 What rituals of the church help you to practise hope when hope feels distant?

2 Where do you see God working in your community? How does this help you to practise hope?

Lindsay Gray, editorial director

Temptation

Read James 1:13–18

Let us examine our ways and test them, and let us return to the Lord.
Lamentations 3:40 (NIV)

Following my retirement in 2018, I began walking my dog, Annie, every morning. One of our routes takes us past fields and farmland with beautiful mountain ranges in the distance. However, the road also has roller-coaster hills, sharp turns and no shoulder. When we take this route, I cross from one side of the road to the other so we are always visible to traffic. While I know which side of the road is safe, Annie is always drawn to the other side, tempted by what she might find.

How often do we do the same in the course of a day? We may begin our morning in devotion to God and set out to follow the guidance of scripture. But before long we can get caught up in the events around us and give in to the temptations tugging at us – spending money irresponsibly, speaking out of anger, holding on to a grudge, judging a neighbour. It is easy to get drawn in. But scripture reminds us that when we are tempted, God will provide a way out (see 1 Corinthians 10:13). Today, when we feel pulled by temptation, let us examine our ways and return to the Lord.

Prayer: *Forgiving God, when we feel pulled to follow our temptations, help us to return to you. Amen.*

Thought for the day: God will help me overcome temptation.

Debb Bowman (Pennsylvania, USA)

Embraced in God's grace

Read Deuteronomy 33:26–29

The eternal God is your refuge, and underneath are the everlasting arms.
Deuteronomy 33:27 (NIV)

After many years as a stay-at-home mum, I was preparing for an interview. I was anxious, not feeling certain that the Lord wanted me to work outside the home. Just before I left for the interview, the mail arrived. There was an envelope postmarked from the United States. 'Embraced by his grace' was written in the corner of the envelope. My heart jumped. It felt like the Lord was saying it directly to me: 'You are embraced in my grace.'

I opened the envelope and inside were some stickers I had ordered a long time ago. The sender's business card had 2 Corinthians 12:9, my baptism verse, printed on it: 'My grace is sufficient for you.' Her tagline was 'Grace: where our weakness meets God's strength.' She had also included a free sticker that said, 'Follow God's heart.'

In these messages, I felt God whispering to me: 'I embrace you. My grace is still enough for you. My power is made perfect in weakness. Follow my heart.' I went to the interview knowing I walked with God, whatever the outcome. As today's quoted scripture reminds us, 'Underneath are the everlasting arms', and they are arms of grace.

Prayer: *Loving God, may we always know that we are embraced in your grace. In Jesus' name. Amen.*

Thought for the day: Grace is where my weakness meets God's strength.

Jacqueline Day (England, United Kingdom)

The power of an invitation

Read Mark 16:15

'Remember, I am with you always, to the end of the age.'
Matthew 28:20 (NRSV)

No one knows the right time or place to invite people to become a Christian and into the fellowship of the church. Christians must always be open and willing to provide the invitation.

During my mother's funeral the minister told a story about my mother. He said, 'I wouldn't be here today if your mother had not invited me to church.' When the minister was a teenager, our church was having a revival. My mother invited his family to come and sit in the pew with us. This began their regular attendance at our church and later a commitment to become Christians and join the church. This changed his life and later inspired him to become a pastor. My mother's invitation to his family changed his life.

No one knows the time or place that people will be open to an invitation into a fellowship with Christ; as Christians, we must remain open to the possibilities.

Prayer: *Dear God, give us the courage to offer Christ to others. When the opportunity presents itself, help us to be bold and willing. We pray the prayer Jesus taught us, 'Our Father which art in heaven, Hallowed be thy name. Thy kingdom come. Thy will be done, as in heaven, so in earth. Give us day by day our daily bread. And forgive us our sins; for we also forgive every one that is indebted to us. And lead us not into temptation; but deliver us from evil' (Luke 11:2–4, KJV). Amen.*

Thought for the day: One invitation can change a person's life.

James R. Hayes (Tennessee, USA)

Resting in God's love

Read Psalm 56:1–4

When I am afraid, I put my trust in you.
Psalm 56:3 (NRSV)

As I sat down in the hospital waiting room, I hoped that everything would go well with my father's surgery. The doctor had said that it was not a serious procedure, but my anxiety began to increase as time wore on. As I waited, I prayed. I found great relief when I entrusted my father's life to God. Even so, two more hours passed until the doctor came to tell me the surgery had been successful.

During this time I learned to rely fully on God. When fear and anxiety want to grow in our hearts – even when the shadow of death looms near – resting in God's love will refresh us and bring us strength and comfort.

Let's not give fear a chance to control us. God is greater than all our fears and anxiety. When we surrender our worries to God, we can find our burdens lifted and rest in the assurance that God is always with us. Through each struggle that life may bring, God's goodness and protection surround us. Knowing this, we can trust in God's care through all our days.

Prayer: *Dear God, so much in life can make us fearful. Teach us to lay our struggles at your feet, trusting that you will bring the comfort we need to live joyful lives. Amen.*

Thought for the day: When fear surrounds me, I will lean on God's love.

Kumalawaty Sundari (Jakarta, Indonesia)

Daily exercise

Read Matthew 7:24–27

The winds blew and beat against that house; yet it did not fall.
Matthew 7:25 (NIV)

I saw a commercial on TV advertising an exercise gadget. It showed models with perfect abdominal muscles and promised that I, too, could get in great shape if I bought this little contraption and used it – just five minutes a day, twice per week. For 15 years, I've exercised two hours a day, five days a week, so I know there's no quick and easy way to get in shape.

This reminded me of how, after becoming a Christian, I thought all I had to do was go to church on Sundays and that would get my life in shape. But after years of doing this, I saw no real results. I still behaved mostly the same. I still had little peace and joy. And when going through hard times, my faith would crumble. Then I decided to commit to studying the Bible, and God opened my eyes.

I realised that simply going to church isn't enough to build my faith. I need to exercise it daily by praying, reading and studying the Bible, and putting Christ's teachings into practice in my life. After more than ten years of doing this, my behaviour looks godlier. I am full of peace and joy, and I can withstand the storms of life.

Prayer: *Dear Father, help us to be doers of your word, not just hearers. Amen.*

Thought for the day: When we exercise our faith daily, we grow stronger spiritually.

George T. Wilkerson (Maryland, USA)

A living experience

Read John 15:1–8

The word of God is alive and active.
Hebrews 4:12 (NIV)

A few years ago, my younger son sent me the book *Walden* by Henry David Thoreau. Gradually, I worked at reading it through. However, it was a huge effort. Then, this past May, I visited my son. We went to Walden Pond and walked through the woods (actually he pushed me in a wheelchair) to experience the area Thoreau wrote about. We visited the replica of his cabin, witnessing its simplicity in the midst of the majestic woods. When we returned home, I picked up *Walden* again. As I began reading, the book came alive because I had been there.

The Holy Spirit revealed to me in this experience a similarity to when I used to pick up my Bible and make an effort to read it; however, it felt foreign, vague and difficult to comprehend. Then one day I accepted Jesus as my Saviour, asking him to come into my heart. The next time I read my Bible, it came alive to me and has remained the bread of life for me in the decades since. This living experience of scripture is possible when we personally come to know Jesus, who is the Word of God.

Prayer: *Dear God, thank you for the gift of scripture. Help us to grow in our relationship with you as we read your holy words. Amen.*

Thought for the day: The words of scripture come alive when we put them into action.

Margarete Cayford (Washington, USA)

Finding encouragement

Read 1 Samuel 30:1–8

David was greatly distressed; for the people spake of stoning him, because the soul of all the people was grieved, every man for his sons and for his daughters: but David encouraged himself in the Lord his God.

1 Samuel 30:6 (KJV)

After high school, I had high hopes for my continued education because I passed the university entrance exams. To my surprise, however, I wasn't on the list of candidates for my preferred school. I had prayed and trusted God, but my expectations were dashed and discouragement set in. I was also upset because a friend who had earned a lower score was accepted. Angry with God, my faith became weak, and I stopped attending our local church.

However, I heard a sermon that changed my perspective. The preacher talked about one of the difficult times in David's life and emphasised that despite all that befell David, 'He encouraged himself in the Lord his God.' He was at risk of being stoned, yet he did not give up on God. Thinking of David's response, I felt ashamed of how I reacted to my problem.

I learned that God wants us to encourage ourselves during our difficult times. If we hurry off in anger, we might not learn what God is trying to teach us. Even when we feel discouraged or distressed, we can follow David's example and encourage ourselves in the Lord. Doing so demonstrates our true trust in God.

Prayer: *Dear God, give us the grace to learn from our challenges. Help us to encourage ourselves through scripture and our relationship with you. Amen.*

Thought for the day: When challenges arise, I will seek encouragement in God.

Ehi Ogwiji (Federal Capital Territory, Nigeria)

Wind and waves

Read Matthew 14:22–33

But when he saw the wind, he was afraid and, beginning to sink, cried out, 'Lord, save me!'
Matthew 14:30 (NIV)

For a while in my life, I struggled with anxiety. It had become so bad that it was difficult for me to visit the local supermarket for groceries and other necessities. Usually, I would just grit my teeth and push through, but sometimes the fear became overwhelming. It seemed silly to fear something so mundane, especially in comparison to the bravery of Peter as he stepped out on to the waves. Forget jumping out of a boat! I could hardly take a stroll down aisle 9 for laundry detergent.

I found it comforting to know that even brave people like Peter can fall when facing frightful wind and waves. But ultimately, it wasn't Peter's bravery that helped me conquer my own fears. It was realising that what truly mattered was that he kept his eyes on Christ. It wasn't until Peter took his eyes off Jesus, focusing on the things to fear, that he began to sink. Admittedly, that's when I begin to sink into my fears as well.

Through Christ, I have come a long way in my anxiety and have made strides I never thought possible. I do my best to focus on Christ rather than the wind and waves and take comfort that he will be there to catch me if I fall. Christ will always be there to save us, no matter the storm.

Prayer: *Father in heaven, in you we can do all things and overcome any obstacle. Help us to keep our eyes firmly focused on you. Amen.*

Thought for the day: Through Christ, I can overcome all my fears.

Carl Bromley (Texas, USA)

Breath of life

Read Ezekiel 36:33–38

The desolate land will be cultivated instead of lying desolate in the sight of all who pass through it.
Ezekiel 36:34 (NIV)

Where I live, the weather can be very humid, but our plants are accustomed to it. On the other hand, the winter season can be very cruel. This year, during a particularly cold season, my plants were devastated. The patio where I keep almost all my plants looked like a wasteland. At a glance, they looked dead. I began to cut the dry twigs and stems, though I wondered if any of this work was worth it. When I came to my favourite plant, I saw what I thought were the tiniest sprouts on the side of each dry stem. Thinking I might be mistaken, I took a closer look. Lo and behold, I could see the miracle of life. The plant was greening – slowly but surely.

I paused to reflect on parallels in my own life. How many times have I walked through a spiritual desert alone, almost lifeless, bereft of hope? Yet, somewhere deep in the innermost part of my heart, the Lord always offers whispers of hope. The ways of the Lord are beyond my understanding, but what I do know is that it is the Lord who infuses new life in me. Where there is life, there is hope. God is the life source – ever-present and working miracles in us and through us.

Prayer: *Giver of life, in the desolate seasons of life, surround us with your presence. When it appears that all is lost, renew our hope. Amen.*

Thought for the day: God's breath of life can transform a desolate season into a season of hope.

Samanta Santillán (Córdoba, Argentina)

Like an eagle

Read Romans 8:18–30

They that wait upon the Lord shall renew their strength; they shall mount up with wings as eagles; they shall run, and not be weary; and they shall walk, and not faint.

Isaiah 40:31 (KJV)

A cacophony of crows drew my eyes heavenward. A dozen or more were flying above a bald eagle, taking turns diving at the eagle's head. It made me think about the pressures of ministry that were barraging me. When I had to dismiss a volunteer, it caused a ripple of dissent within the ministry. Friends were calling me to offer their advice. But I felt harassed and weary.

Above my head, the eagle appeared not to notice the annoying crows. Its speed and altitude never changed when the crows swooped within inches of its head. The eagle continued to fly a straight course. I wanted to be like that eagle, to remain swift and unfazed. I was reminded of today's quoted scripture: 'They that wait upon the Lord shall renew their strength; they shall mount up with wings as eagles.' I closed my eyes to sit in God's presence, and God assured me that I had done the right thing. When I opened my eyes a few minutes later, I felt confident and able to face any challenge.

Spending time in God's presence renews our strength when we feel harassed or weary. With God's help, we can move forward with speed and endurance like an eagle.

Prayer: *Thank you, Father, for the peace of your presence. You give us the strength and hope to rise above. Amen.*

Thought for the day: When I spend time with God, my strength is renewed.

Cindy W. Arora (Washington, USA)

Love never fails

Read 1 Corinthians 13:1–8

Love never fails. But where there are prophecies, they will cease; where there are tongues, they will be stilled; where there is knowledge, it will pass away.
1 Corinthians 13:8 (NIV)

One day I was feeling lonely and discouraged. I was struggling with unemployment and felt like no one cared about me. I decided to go for a walk to clear my mind, and I noticed a beautiful flower by the side of the road. It was bright yellow with delicate petals and looked like a ray of sunshine amid the grey day. I felt a surge of joy and gratitude as I admired it. God had sent me this sign, reminding me of God's love and presence. God had not forgotten or abandoned me.

I thought of 1 Corinthians 13, which describes God's love. It is patient and kind. It does not remember the bad things we do. It never fails. This reminder comforted and encouraged me. I decided to trust God more and share God's love with others.

I picked the flower and gave it to a passing stranger. She smiled and thanked me. I felt a connection with her and with God. God loves us with an everlasting love that never fails.

Prayer: *Dear God, thank you for your unfailing love. Help us to recognise the signs of your love that surround us each day and to share them with others. Amen.*

Thought for the day: God's love is like a flower that brightens my day and fills my heart with joy.

A. Ngamshing (Nagaland, India)

Holy tears

Read James 5:13–16

Whatever you do, do it from the heart for the Lord and not for people.
Colossians 3:23 (CEB)

Due to our lead pastor's absence one Sunday, the associate pastor asked several lay members to help with various roles during the worship service. I was asked to lead the congregational prayer time. Prayer is such an intimate and often emotional experience for me that I sometimes have difficulty holding back tears during prayer. Even so, I agreed.

At the appointed time, I stepped boldly to the podium, feeling confident I could keep my composure. I had uttered only a few words of humble praise, however, when my voice trembled and my chin quivered. Sure enough, tears escaped from my closed eyelids, and the tears flowed harder the more I prayed. Somehow I managed to finish with the Lord's Prayer and make it back to my pew, but I felt remorseful and embarrassed by my public display.

Then I remembered that God doesn't demand a performance from me. God wants me to serve with my whole heart. Emotions are real and God-given, and tears can be a kind of holy water. Our creator made me with a tender heart. It doesn't matter what others think or say about my prayerful tears. Perhaps that day wasn't my shining moment, but it was God's.

Prayer: *Almighty God, we are thankful that we have constant access to you through the power of prayer. Amen.*

Thought for the day: It is a humbling privilege to pray before almighty God.

Wilma R. Vernich (Tennessee, USA)

Our protector

Read Job 42:12–17

'My Spirit, who is on you, will not depart from you, and my words that I have put in your mouth will always be on your lips.'
Isaiah 59:21 (NIV)

I work on a vegetable farm. There are times of the year when strong winds can erode our soil and stunt or kill younger shoots. To prevent this, we plant narrow strips of grain before we plant the vegetables. The grain germinates and grows a few inches tall, and then we plant the vegetables. The grain acts as a windbreak for the vegetables, protecting the tiny plants as they emerge from the soil. Sometimes the wind blows so much soil up against the grain that it looks like a snow drift.

In our lives we often face adversities that cause fear, anxiety, tension, anger or frustration. But like the grain strips, God provides us with a hedge of protection. For Balaam, God's protection was in the form of a donkey (see Numbers 22:21–33). Job endured intense hardship, but God blessed him in his later years with a season of prosperity. As Christians, we believe Jesus' promise to us in John 14:16: 'I will ask the Father, and he will give you another advocate to help you and be with you forever.' God is our protector and helper through life's storms.

Prayer: *Dear God, thank you for helping us. Give us strength to endure the difficult seasons of our lives. Amen.*

Thought for the day: God is my protector and helper.

Phil Reynolds (South Carolina, USA)

By faith

Read 1 Peter 1:1–9

These have come so that the proven genuineness of your faith – of greater worth than gold, which perishes even though refined by fire – may result in praise, glory and honour when Jesus Christ is revealed.
1 Peter 1:7 (NIV)

The day my first child, Rex Isaiah, was born was also the day he passed away. He was born at 25 weeks gestation due to complications and spent three hours intubated in the NICU before going to be with the Lord. My husband and I wrestled with our new reality, reeling from shock and grief. For a while I surrendered to the lament in my soul and voiced my anguish to God. In the wake of Rex's death, my husband and I plumbed the depths of our faith.

Loss tests us and gives rise to difficult questions. Why did God allow this to happen? Why didn't God answer our prayers? How do we continue after our hope has been dashed?

The Christian walk is not for the faint-hearted. Our understanding of God's goodness cannot hinge upon answered prayers and joyful testimonies alone. We are called to a substantial faith where we invest our heart, mind and soul. Our faith bears the weight of afflictions. Faith in Christ helps us to trust that the Lord is good and to persevere through the darkest hours. It provides an assurance of God's promises – of a future we cannot see but hold on to in hope.

Prayer: *Dear Father, teach us to put our faith in you alone. As we endure suffering and loss, help us maintain our faith and hope in you. Guide us as we persevere. Amen.*

Thought for the day: A faith rooted in Christ can bear the weight of life's afflictions.

Piyumi Kapugeekiyana (England, United Kingdom)

A godmother's example

Read Matthew 25:31–40

Whatever you do, do it from the heart for the Lord and not for people.
Colossians 3:23 (CEB)

My godmother taught me many things, both in what she said and in what she did. She lived simply without modern gadgets, and she was a wise, contented person. Her husband, my uncle, was a full-time youth worker who regularly took groups of teenagers away to weekend camps.

It quite often rained at these camps and my uncle would return looking rather bedraggled. After one such weekend, I noticed my godmother washing my uncle's muddy socks at the kitchen sink. 'I used to hate this job,' she told me, 'and then I thought, *What if these were Jesus' muddy socks? I'd so gladly wash them for him.* And now that makes all the difference.'

My godmother's words have come back to me several times since, especially when I am faced with a task I would rather not do. When I stop and remember that I can work as if Jesus is on the receiving end of what I do, it gives me special joy.

Prayer: *Lord, thank you that in serving others we are serving you. What an encouragement and privilege! We pray as you taught us: 'Our Father who is in heaven, uphold the holiness of your name. Bring in your kingdom so that your will is done on earth as it's done in heaven. Give us the bread we need for today. Forgive us for the ways we have wronged you, just as we also forgive those who have wronged us. And don't lead us into temptation, but rescue us from the evil one' (Matthew 6:9–13). Amen.*

Thought for the day: Even the humblest task can be done for the Lord.

Elaine Brown (Scotland, United Kingdom)

New strength

Read Matthew 26:36–46

It is God who arms me with strength and keeps my way secure.
Psalm 18:32 (NIV)

It was a terrible night. Something had triggered the memory of hurts from long ago. I couldn't fall asleep as I replayed these crushing experiences in my mind. Since I couldn't sleep, I read Matthew 26:36–46, which describes Jesus' agonising prayers in the garden of Gethsemane.

Strangely, I was comforted that Jesus' closest friends – Peter, James and John – couldn't support him because they fell asleep. This prompted me to go back to bed, and thankfully I slept another few hours.

But when I woke up at 6.00 am, I could hardly stand. My wife and I had to leave soon for church, since I was in the choir. I worried that in this wobbly state I wouldn't be able to sing. Then I remembered a verse from a psalm I had read a few days before: 'It is God who arms me with strength and keeps my way secure.' In the midst of troubles, God gave David strength. A sense of calm came over me, and I felt a new vigour, trusting that what God had done for David, God would do for me.

Prayer: *Merciful God, when we feel completely drained, thank you for giving us strength. Amen.*

Thought for the day: When I ask for help, God will renew my strength.

Wolfgang Bernhardt (KwaZulu-Natal, South Africa)

God remembers

Read Genesis 8:1–5
God remembered Noah.
Genesis 8:1 (KJV)

I don't live near the ocean, and I have no idea what it feels like to sit in a boat and see nothing but water on the horizon. I do, however, live in the mid-western United States, so during the winter my skyline often disappears into infinite snow. It's a lonely time – a time of waiting. And it makes me think about Noah's plight. The Bible says the water covered the earth for many months. That's months of sitting in a boat, looking at an empty horizon. Months of feeling vulnerable, of drifting, of waiting on God.

I wonder if Noah ever cried out like the psalmist, 'Has God forgotten to be merciful?' (Psalm 77:9, NIV).

Often the ordeals of this life seem to drag on and on. Sometimes when the stark horizon shows no sign of changing, like so many faithful people in the Bible we cry out in anguish to God. But the Bible is also full of passages like Genesis 8:1: 'God remembered Noah.'

Even people of faith need to hear that God will never leave them, forsake them or forget them. God remembered Noah, and God will remember you and me.

Prayer: *Dear God, hear our cry for help. Thank you for stories from scripture that strengthen us. Remind us that Noah's floodwaters did not last forever. Amen.*

Thought for the day: Waiting for God doesn't mean God has forgotten me.

Geo PicKell (North Dakota, USA)

Excited to serve

Read Philippians 2:12–18
It is God who works in you to will and to act in order to fulfil his good purpose.
Philippians 2:13 (NIV)

As I planned the upcoming meeting of our Christian fellowship group, I gave one friend the job of welcoming people as they arrived. Following our meeting, I received a message from her: 'Sister,' she said, 'can I take on this ministry again next week? I loved doing it.'

Welcoming people is a simple ministry, but my friend was excited to do it. I could see in her heart that she would do whatever she could to be the hands of God.

That same desire was in the apostle Paul's heart, even in prison. The letters he wrote while in prison have blessed generations of people.

The desire to serve God grows out of the belief that 'It is God who works in [us] to will and to act in order to fulfil his good purpose.' If we can embrace the same excitement and desire to serve God as did my friend in our fellowship group, we will be doing fruitful labour for God. God entrusts to us many opportunities for service. Following my friend's example, whatever work I can do for God, I will be excited to do!

Prayer: *Dear God, continue to show us that our lives are filled with opportunities to reveal your love and purpose to your people. May we serve joyfully. Through Christ, our Lord. Amen.*

Thought for the day: Today I will be ready to serve God with joy.

Linawati Santoso (East Java, Indonesia)

The church in the sky

Read 1 Peter 2:9–10
'Where two or three gather in my name, there am I with them.'
Matthew 18:20 (NIV)

My younger son, Kris, worships at an independent Christian church in New York City. They originally rented a space on the 40th floor of a building in Manhattan. It had an amazing view of the city from floor-to-ceiling windows. Each week they would set up for Sunday school and take their resources out of a locked closet. One Sunday they had the kids draw pictures of what a church looked like. The next week they posted pictures in the foyer. I was amazed that all the kids drew pictures of skyscrapers with a special room on top. I would never have imagined a skyscraper church, but the children did.

This was not at all my idea of church, and so different from the one where I grew up – a modest white clapboard building with limited seating for 100 and an adjacent fellowship hall.

But Matthew reminds us that the church is more about the people than the building. 'Where two or three gather' Christ will be there, no matter what the building looks like. What will the church look like in the future? I am not sure, but I know God will be with us.

Prayer: *Dear God of all, thank you for your promise to be with us where two or three are gathered. Help us to be open to new ideas of what church might look like. Amen.*

Thought for the day: What will the church of the future look like?

Mike Bertoglio (Georgia, USA)

Be still

Read Psalm 46

'Be still, and know that I am God; I will be exalted among the nations, I will be exalted in the earth.'
Psalm 46:10 (NIV)

In August 2021, I began a months-long healing journey following spinal surgery. I had to stop working and to alter many activities in order to heal properly. My heart was in a hurry to recover so that I could get back to my regular life, but my body was clearly letting me know that this would take time. Part of my physical therapy included walking in my neighbourhood, which became spiritual therapy as well.

During one of my daily walks, I noticed a flock of egrets standing serenely in the marsh grass preening. I stopped to watch and be still with them. Suddenly, without taking a step, one of the birds gracefully bent his neck towards the water and picked up a passing fish. Then I noticed another egret walking briskly through the marsh, his long neck oddly bent with one eye towards the water. He seemed to be frantically searching for a fish.

The contrast between the two egrets was stark, and I felt God speaking to me, telling me to be still and trust that the healing I needed would come in good time. I should not be like that frantic egret. During the following months I have found God to be faithful, and I have done my best to be still and receive.

Prayer: *Dear Lord, help us to be still and wait on you. Even when we do not understand the journey, we trust that you will provide what we need for our good and for your glory. Amen.*

Thought for the day: God is faithful, and I can trust God to provide for my good.

Frances Grainger Keller (South Carolina, USA)

The narrow way

Read Matthew 7:13–14

'The gate is narrow and the road is hard that leads to life,
and there are few who find it.'
Matthew 7:14 (NRSV)

Recently, my son and I were driving in the Scottish Highlands. The shift to driving on the left really tested my reflexes. Miles and miles of single lane roads with sometimes short and narrow passing places created a new challenge to my American instincts. On one-lane roads my instinct was to pull to the right, which once nearly ended in disaster.

After that frightful incident, my son insisted that every time we came to a passing place I should pull left even if no car was approaching. I initially resisted his suggestion, but I decided to humour him. I started swerving into every passing place on the left. The more I swerved left, the more instinctive the motion became and the less thought was required. That day's trip brought a sense of increased mastery of a life-saving habit.

How often do we assume that because we've had an experience or know how to do something we don't necessarily need to develop a regular pattern of practice? We basically know what the Bible says. Maybe we've read it from cover to cover. We made a profession of faith. We go to church. We pray. Isn't that enough? What are we missing by our failure to develop regular practices of devotion: stewardship, corporate and personal Bible study, prayer, public and private worship?

Prayer: *Dear Jesus, your words make us uncomfortable. Help us to get past our discomfort so we can recognise the resources you provide for the road ahead. Amen.*

Thought for the day: What aspect of my faith do I need to practise today?

Torrey Curtis (Oklahoma, USA)

A change of attitude

Read Romans 5:1–5

*Consider it pure joy, my brothers and sisters, whenever you face
trials of many kinds, because you know that the testing of your faith
produces perseverance.*
James 1:2–3 (NIV)

In 2017, after completing my internship, my life took an unfortunate turn:
I was diagnosed with chronic fatigue syndrome. Because it would be a
lifelong condition, I kept asking God, 'Why?' Months after the diagnosis,
I carried the same negative attitude. Every day was filled with crying, anger
and feelings of hopelessness. I felt so fatigued that walking became a problem. Because I could not sleep at night, my brain function deteriorated.

Through this trial my faith was tested. But I drew closer to God and
changed my 'poor-me' attitude. Yes, struggles come with pain and suffering, but hoping and trusting in God gives us the courage to endure
our trials confidently.

In today's scripture, James tells us to consider it joy when facing trials.
The joy – the hope – I had was that healing would come for me. Now, one
year later, my symptoms have improved and I rarely lose sleep.

As we face challenges, let's ask God to help us change our attitude
and to let hope grow within us.

Prayer: *Dear God, give us hope as we endure the struggles that our
life brings. Change our attitude from sorrow to joy, knowing you will
see us through. Amen.*

Thought for the day: A positive attitude towards trials allows God's
joy to help me heal.

Hedina Ojwang (Nakuru County, Kenya)

Broken shells

Read Psalm 34:15–22

The Lord is close to the brokenhearted and saves those who are crushed in spirit.
Psalm 34:18 (NIV)

I love to walk the beach and look for seashells. Sometimes the shells I spot in the sand are only fragments, and I usually toss the broken pieces back into the ocean and continue my search. On a recent visit to the beach, I found a pearlescent shell. But when I dug it out of the sand, I saw that it was broken. As I went to toss the shell away, I hesitated and placed it in my pocket instead.

It came to my mind then that we often 'toss away' our brothers and sisters too. Sometimes we are too distracted or unwilling to acknowledge someone's broken spirit, attitude or physical appearance. We toss them aside rather than looking deeper and offering prayer, assistance or an encouraging word. There have been many times I could have helped someone on the street, offered an encouraging word or taken time to deliver meals to others. Instead I went about my day worried only about my own to-do list.

I believe God spoke to me on the beach that day. I resolved to see the beauty in broken seashells. And beyond that, I hope to be more open every day to how I may reach out to those around me.

Prayer: *Dear Lord, open our eyes to the brokenness in the world around us so we may see the ways we can help. Guide us to act when we see someone in need. Amen.*

Thought for the day: Today I will look for ways I can help those who are hurting.

Barb Baylor Anderson (South Carolina, USA)

Good intentions

Read Jeremiah 29:10–14

I know the plans I have for you, says the Lord, plans for your welfare and not for harm, to give you a future with hope.
Jeremiah 29:11 (NRSV)

We have dense scrub at the edges of our property, and feral cats pose a danger to the many native animals and birds that reside here. So we set out humane traps to catch and remove them. However, we often find a native animal – perhaps an echidna or a currawong – caught in the trap and awaiting release.

One morning, a trap had caught a powerful Rosenberg's goanna. As I approached the trap to release the lizard, he opened his jaws wide. Thrashing about in the cage, he hissed and glared at me. He was terrified of me, and every effort I made to release him made him more hostile. After I finally managed to open the trap, I left him alone to find his way out in his own time.

How often do we similarly fail to understand that God's only intention is to help us? We may fear God's tender and loving approach and struggle against it because we don't realise that all God wants is to love us and set us free. As the prophet Jeremiah reminds us, God's intention is not to harm but to prosper us; to release us from our captivity and from all fear.

Prayer: *Thank you, loving God, for your unwavering love for us at all times. Help us to entrust ourselves fully to your love and to remember that your only intention is to bless us. Amen.*

Thought for the day: I can trust that God desires only my good.

Dorothy O'Neill (South Australia, Australia)

Two words

Read 1 Kings 18:22–39

'When you pray, do not keep on babbling like pagans, for they think they will be heard because of their many words.'
Matthew 6:7 (NIV)

It's been over 50 years, but I still remember my sixth-grade Sunday school class like it was yesterday. That's because it changed how I experienced church and how I prayed. After spending years in basement classrooms, I moved to the sixth-grade classroom, which was up in the steeple of the church. And the class was taught by a man – the first male teacher I had ever had.

His lesson on prayer has stayed with me all my life. He recounted a time when he was driving on an icy, country road and his car spun out of control and careened towards a tree. He told us that he prayed a two-word prayer: 'Not now.' Though he didn't have time to embellish his prayer with formalities, God heard his prayer.

In 1 Kings 18, the prophets of Baal thought they would be heard because of their many words. When God's prophet Elijah prayed, his prayer was only a couple of sentences long, yet God heard him and answered his prayer. We don't need to concoct long, fancy prayers in order to pray. From the first syllables we utter, God listens to us.

Prayer: *Whether our prayers are long or short, you, O Lord, hear the cries of our heart. We thank you for your constant presence with us. As Jesus taught us, we pray, 'Father, hallowed be your name, your kingdom come. Give us each day our daily bread. Forgive us our sins, for we also forgive everyone who sins against us. And lead us not into temptation' (Luke 11:2–4). Amen.*

Thought for the day: No matter how I pray, God hears me.

David R. Schultz (Illinois, USA)

God never fails

Read Psalm 121

Each of you should use whatever gift you have received to serve others, as faithful stewards of God's grace in its various forms.
1 Peter 4:10 (NIV)

I started journalling 23 years ago on my 50th birthday. Each year, I fill a journal with my thoughts and feelings about daily life. It helps me de-stress and keep track of major events in my life.

On my birthday, I add a gratitude list to that year's journal. After completing the list, I go back to the first journal and read every journal I have. The pages contain discussions of what I've experienced, God's presence, gratitude, praise reports and prayer requests. I am always astounded to see so many prayers answered, and I feel God's faithfulness, love and mercy anew.

Reading the journals also makes me feel better about aging. I focus on what I can still do instead of the discomfort and changes in ability that have come with aging. I see where I have helped others and tried to be God's hands and feet. This always lifts my spirits because it reflects 1 Peter 4:10, 'Each of you should use whatever gift you have received to serve others.' My journals remind me of all the good God has done in my life, the blessings God has helped me provide for others, and God's presence with me always.

Prayer: *Gracious God, help us to see and feel your presence and to show your grace and love to everyone we meet. In the name of Jesus Christ we pray. Amen.*

Thought for the day: With God's help, I will use my blessings to serve others.

Janis Gregg Pressley (Maryland, USA)

Fully equipped

Read 1 Samuel 17:38–50

David fastened on his sword over the tunic and tried walking around, because he was not used to them. 'I cannot go in these,' he said to Saul, 'because I am not used to them.' So he took them off.
1 Samuel 17:39 (NIV)

I am a teacher and a sports coach, and my wife had our first child a few days before the start of the school year. Taking care of a newborn – who seemed to be nocturnal – while also trying to teach and coach left me beyond overwhelmed. As a new father, I've struggled with imposter syndrome. It's hard to be a good father, husband, teacher and coach. It's been exhausting.

At the end of every sports practice, we do a prayer spotlight. One day my players spotlighted me, thanking me and assuring me that my work wasn't going unnoticed. My students reminded me of my purpose and why I do what I do.

Today's scripture reading reminds me that God is our strength and that we can trust that God has equipped us for the purpose God has called us to. Each of us has been given unique attributes, strengths and gifts from God. Psalm 139:14 reminds us that we are 'fearfully and wonderfully made'. God has given us what we need, and we can trust God to see us through.

Prayer: *Dear God, help us to trust you and to use the unique gifts and talents that you have equipped us with to glorify you. Amen.*

Thought for the day: I will trust that God has equipped me for my journey.

Dalton Haist (Kansas, USA)

Past and present

Read 1 John 2:15–17
The world and its desires pass away, but whoever does the will of God lives forever.
1 John 2:17 (NIV)

'You'll never guess what I've found,' my husband said. 'These are local newspapers from when I was young.' He had been helping his mother clear out her house for renovating. The newspapers, which my late father-in-law had kept, were from the 1980s and 1990s. Each one included a photograph of my husband as a boy – on a team, on a trip or from a key event that had happened in the town's history.

Reading the newspapers transported us back to the past. The articles showed how the cost of living had changed. Even the printing and layout were antiquated compared to today's standards. But more than anything, they reminded me that each moment is precious. Our dreams and desires – even our worries – slip by so quickly. The old anxieties we had about school, exams and growing up are no longer relevant. What still matters is the relationship we have with our loving God.

This experience reminded me to value each day and to be thankful for the years we have been given. We can make a difference in our lives and in the lives of others by spending time with God, cherishing those around us and doing kind deeds – no matter how small.

Prayer: *Dear God, help us to remember how precious our time is and to appreciate it. Show us how to reach out to those in need. Amen.*

Thought for the day: Today is a gift from God, and I will be thankful.

Cindy Lee (England, United Kingdom)

Praying with

Read Philippians 4:4–7

Do not be anxious about anything, but in everything by prayer and supplication with thanksgiving let your requests be made known to God.

Philippians 4:6 (NRSV)

As a hospital administrator, I often pray with patients to offer them comfort and peace. Recently, I encountered an elderly man who is a very familiar face in our community. He was a successful businessman. Before I left his room, I asked if I could pray for him. He smiled, so I proceeded to pray. At the conclusion of my prayer, he looked at me with tears in his eyes and said, 'No one has ever prayed for me before.' How can this be? I thought to myself. Surely someone along his life's journey had prayed for him from a distance. Praying to God we often specifically name people, but how often do we go to those persons and pray with them? How much more powerful it would have been if someone had stopped for a moment and prayed with this man!

As Christians, we are to be the hands and feet as well as the eyes and ears of Christ. Each of us in our daily prayers can continue to pray for people – and pray with them as well.

Prayer: *Loving God, be with us today as we encourage one another by praying together for your will to be done in our lives. Amen.*

Thought for the day: Prayer has the power to connect me to God and to others.

Ronda Lehman (Ohio, USA)

My source

Read Matthew 6:25–34

*'Do not worry about tomorrow, for tomorrow will worry about itself.
Each day has enough trouble of its own.'*
Matthew 6:34 (NIV)

I was feeling lost and alone, struggling with my faith and feeling unsure of my purpose. I had been going through a time of distress, dealing with financial complications and strained relationships. One night, overwhelmed and desperate for guidance, I opened the Bible and came across Matthew 6:25–34.

Reading that passage, I realised that I had been focusing too much on my problems and not enough on my faith. I had been worrying about things that were beyond my control and had lost sight of the fact that God was with me and would provide me with better possibilities. I took the passage to heart and started to focus on my relationship with God, praying and meditating on God's word. Over time, I felt more peace and contentment, and I began to see a way through my difficulties.

The Bible can provide relief and direction during trying times, and concentrating on our faith can help us find peace and determination. So let us prioritise our relationship with God every day, believing in God's provision and guidance. No matter our circumstances, we can make time for prayer and reflection and focus on God's word as a source of well-being and relief.

Prayer: *Dear God, thank you for providing for us during times of crisis. We trust in your goodness and love to guide us through any challenge. Amen.*

Thought for the day: Faith in God's word provides direction during trying times.

Ryan J. Kingsman (Punjab, Pakistan)

Help from my friends

Read James 3:5–13

A friend loves at all times, and a brother is born for a time of adversity.
Proverbs 17:17 (NIV)

One day I posted some remarks on social media that I thought were pretty innocuous. When I checked back several hours later, someone had added an angry comment condemning me. However, following that comment, two others defended me and vouched for my character. Both were people I knew from high school – many, many years ago. While we were friends online, we had not met in person for quite some time. And yet, they stood up for me in a kind and supportive way. Their words took the sting out of that negative post.

Our words have power either to build up or tear down. Harsh, condemning words can damage a fragile soul, bring anger and retribution, and cause division. They can destroy Christians' witness to the world and repel those who might have come to Christ.

On the other hand, words spoken in love can give hope to the hurting, heal emotional wounds and give strength to the weary. They can draw people to our loving God. As representatives of Christ, let's consider our words carefully so that we accurately witness to God's grace and mercy. Our words can make a difference.

Prayer: *Dear Lord, thank you for the grace you have given us. Help us to speak words of grace and mercy and teach us to stand up for those who are unfairly judged. Amen.*

Thought for the day: Today I will speak words of grace.

Susan Thogerson Maas (Oregon, USA)

Hearing God's voice

Read Exodus 3:1–4

God called to him from within the bush, 'Moses! Moses!'
Exodus 3:4 (NIV)

The walls of our old house are thin. I often hear the sounds of the city outside and of people passing by – a child crying, a couple with slightly raised voices, a group of giggling school children. These background noises have become a part of my everyday life, and I hardly acknowledge them. But every once in a while something comes through clearly.

Throughout our lives, almost in the background, God speaks to us – in the wise words of others, in scripture, in our circumstances and surroundings. It is rare that we hear the voice of God clearly like Moses did. Moses was going about his daily work of shepherding when he noticed an unusual sight – a burning bush – and then heard God's call. It was impossible to ignore.

God speaks to us too. God never ceases speaking, and taking time to stop, pray and listen to God is an essential discipline in our Christian life. Often it is easy to neglect wise advice, to let our eyes pass over our daily scripture reading without really paying attention, to fail to notice those in need around us or God's blessings surrounding us. Let us remember to pause and notice what God is saying to us.

Prayer: *Dear Lord, help us to notice when you are speaking to us today. Thank you for surrounding us with your presence. Amen.*

Thought for the day: Today I will pause and listen for God's voice.

Sarah Kelleth (Tokyo, Japan)

Power in weakness

Read 2 Corinthians 12:1–10

'My grace is sufficient for you, for power is made perfect in weakness.'
2 Corinthians 12:9 (NRSV)

For seven years as a child, I took piano lessons. I quickly learned my strength was sight-reading music; and to my annoyance, my weakness was my inability to memorise easily. One year, when the day of the recital came, I still did not feel comfortable with my music. As I walked towards the piano, my stomach was queasy and my hands shaky. I sat down and began to play, but near the end my mind went blank. I could not remember how to finish the piece. Finally, desperate, I just hit a chord, stood up and walked back to my seat, feeling embarrassed.

I wish I could say I overcame my challenges with memorisation. I cannot. I wish I could say I can preach and teach without notes in front of me. I cannot. And yet, God still calls me to teach and occasionally to preach and blesses me despite my weakness.

The Bible has many stories about people who felt inadequate whom God used in powerful ways: Moses and Jeremiah are two examples. Even Mary, Peter and Paul struggled until God's grace saw them through to accomplish powerful works.

When we give our weaknesses as well as our strengths to God, we can stand strong and watch what God does with our lives.

Prayer: *O Lord, use our strengths and weaknesses to glorify you wherever we go, in whatever we do and with whomever we meet. Amen.*

Thought for the day: God can use all that I am to accomplish great things.

Margie McNeir (Texas, USA)

New life

Read Isaiah 43:16–21

Jesus said to her, 'I am the resurrection and the life. Those who believe in me, even though they die, will live.'
John 11:25 (NRSV)

Where I live, we celebrate the resurrection of our Lord in the springtime. The story of Easter is powerful no matter what season of year it is when we celebrate, but the theme of Easter goes particularly well with the theme of spring. The dormancy, cold and bleakness of winter mirrors the body of Christ being in the tomb and the feelings his followers must have experienced. They must have thought all was lost and hope was gone.

When I look out at a winter landscape with bare trees, brown grass and a dark sky, sometimes it's hard to feel excited. But fortunately, spring always comes. Although the transition begins slowly, the trees eventually begin to bud and flowers burst forth. These signs give me hope that new life is coming and put a little bounce in my step, even if I am still wearing winter boots.

The resurrection brought a similar hope. Jesus' lifeless body came back to life. The dark, foreboding tomb was opened, never to be closed again. The morning came alive with the promise of hope returning to earth. God did something new on that Easter morning, and God does something new every spring too.

Prayer: *God of new life, your timing is always perfect. Thank you for the hope of Easter. Amen.*

Thought for the day: In every season, I will hold tight to the hope of new life.

James Golden (Georgia, USA)

Small things matter

Read 1 John 3:16–24

Those who despise a time of little things will rejoice when they see the plumb line in Zerubbabel's hand.
Zechariah 4:10 (CEB)

My brother Tommy was intellectually disabled and lived in a group home. Because I lived in another country, I did not visit him in person. One day I decided to start sending him postcards so he would remember that he had a sister who loved him. I wrote to him regularly. I would choose a nice picture, write out my greeting and send it across the sea.

Tommy passed away some time ago. After his death, the personnel at his group home gave the postcards to my mother. Tommy had saved them. The staff told my mother that Tommy had slept with the postcards under his pillow every night and that he wouldn't let anyone else touch them because they were so precious to him. It moved my heart deeply to know that an action of mine that was so small had meant so much to my brother.

Our lives are full of things that seem inconsequential. While a kind gesture or an encouraging word may not seem noteworthy, they can mean much. God's word encourages us to love, even in little ways. In doing so, we spread the joy of God's kingdom and lives can be changed.

Prayer: *Dear Lord, thank you for opportunities to care for others. Help us to share your love today, even in little ways. Amen.*

Thought for the day: Sharing God's love in small ways can make a big difference.

Carol Westerlund (Uusimaa, Finland)

Known by name

Read Genesis 32:22–32

Don't fear, for I have redeemed you; I have called you by name; you are mine.
Isaiah 43:1 (CEB)

My husband is intentional about asking for someone's name or looking for their name tag and then using it in an encouraging, conversational way. When speaking to a salesclerk, for example, he might say, 'Lily – that reminds me of springtime,' or, 'Jacob – that's a Bible name!' Our names personalise us and are openings to further conversation. My husband's intentionality reminds me that the store clerk I interact with is Sally, who has hopes and dreams of her own. The person who delivers my mail is not a nameless postal carrier but Sam, who has a life, a family and a story.

In the Bible, names especially have meanings that point to the bearer's destiny or purpose or that reflect God's work in their life. For example, Jacob became Israel, Saul changed to Paul and Simon was called Peter. God has shown us that names have value, even in naming his Son.

We are each important, and our individual names reflect our worth. We can recognise the inherent worth of each person – each child of God – by acknowledging and encouraging (by name whenever possible) the people we encounter each day.

Prayer: *Dear Lord, help us to acknowledge each individual we encounter today, remembering that you have created them in your image. Amen.*

Thought for the day: I will respect and encourage each person I encounter.

Susan H. Aaron (Florida, USA)

Accepting God's grace

Read Psalm 51:1–12

Restore to me the joy of your salvation, and sustain in me a willing spirit.
Psalm 51:12 (NRSV)

Psalm 51 speaks to the brokenness of our hearts and our need to turn to the Lord for restoration. This psalm was written by David after he had committed adultery with Bathsheba. David expressed his contrition from the depths of his soul and asked for mercy, forgiveness, grace and love.

We all can relate to the brokenness and shame David expressed in this psalm. Each of us needs God's mercy and grace too. I remember when I first came to the Lord after years of running away. I was filled with guilt and regret, and I was ashamed of my past. I had so much darkness within me. But in Christ I found a profound sense of liberation and peace. I was overwhelmed by the Lord's mercy and kindness, and I knew that I had found a new beginning.

Psalm 51 reminds us that no matter how we have sinned, the Lord is ready to forgive us and restore our relationship. When we approach in repentance, the Lord will meet us with a tenderness and compassion we cannot fathom and will abundantly pour out mercy and grace to us. The Lord receives us with open arms and fills us with love and joy.

Prayer: *Faithful God, thank you for your restoring forgiveness. Come into our hearts and remove desires that are not a part of your plan for us. Amen.*

Thought for the day: Christ offers me forgiveness, mercy and love.

Tess McCumstie (Victoria, Australia)

For everyday use

Read Matthew 22:34–39

I urge you, brothers and sisters, in view of God's mercy, to offer your bodies as a living sacrifice, holy and pleasing to God.
Romans 12:1 (NIV)

A parable that I was told by a Sunday school teacher has stayed with me over the years. It was about a little girl who had been given the most beautiful doll, which came in a box. Every week she would take it out and look at it in wonder, but then put it away again. To her it was not for everyday use. But as a result the doll was never used for what it was made for, to be played with. The point of the story is that our faith is meant for everyday use; it is not just to be taken out and admired once a week.

God wants us to walk with him daily, not just on a Sunday. We are called to wholeheartedly follow God, to love him with all of our heart, soul, mind and strength and not to pay mere lip service. God wants the nitty gritty of our lives, the highs and the lows. Full involvement. A daily life of feeding on God's word and dedicated prayer. Our heavenly Father knows us through and through and has called us to be his hands and feet in this world, so a faith just for Sunday is never going to radiate God's love out in our lives.

Prayer: *Father God, help us to worship you with our whole lives day by day. Thank you for all the ways that you help us with this, in your word and in our prayers. Amen.*

Thought for the day: I can shine the light of God wherever I am.

Hilary Sixsmith (England, United Kingdom)

Trust in the Lord

Read Jeremiah 17:5–10

Blessed are those who trust in the Lord, whose trust is the Lord.
Jeremiah 17:7 (NRSV)

Where I live, we have only two seasons – wet and dry. April and May are usually the hottest months and for the past few weeks we've been experiencing extremely hot days with no rain.

Recently our water source was drying up and my family's water pump stopped working. I read a news headline claiming that we have an 80 percent chance of experiencing the climate pattern known as El Niño in the coming weeks. I was scared by this possibility, because El Niño's warm waters are associated with drought in my country. It was already hotter than we could bear. How much harder would it be without water? What would my family drink?

God surely knows what we need and when we need it. As I was reading my journal, I saw that a few days back I had written down Jeremiah 17:5–10. The passage compares those who trust in man and those who trust in the Lord. Verse 8 says those who trust in the Lord will be like a tree planted by water and will not be anxious when drought comes. This reminded me to trust and fix my eyes and heart on God. Regardless of the changing seasons, I can trust God will remain faithful through it all.

Prayer: *Dear Lord, we know you are faithful and trustworthy. Help us to fix our eyes on you, no matter what we are going through. Amen.*

Thought for the day: I can trust in the Lord amid changing seasons.

Quennie Joyce Ibarra (Cagayan, Philippines)

Words and deeds

Read James 2:14–17

Faith is dead when it doesn't result in faithful activity.
James 2:17 (CEB)

The plane turbulence was moderate, but I'd experienced far worse. However, when I turned to the college-aged person sitting next to me, I saw from the look on her face that she was terrified. I decided to talk to her, explaining what was happening, how long it generally lasted and assuring her that the first time I experienced similar turbulence was unpleasant as well. Gradually, both she and the plane settled. When it was time to descend for landing, we started to experience more turbulence. She asked if I could talk her through everything again. I did.

Sometimes we underestimate the power of words, thinking that only our actions matter in God's eyes. After all, hoping someone will be fed or finds shelter is far different than directly providing for them. Yet I've learned that sometimes our words and our deeds become one and the same. What that young woman needed more than anything was a reassuring voice.

As we were exiting the plane she said, 'I don't know how to thank you.' I told her that I imagined her on an airplane a few decades from now, having become an experienced traveller. I imagined her turning to someone else and helping them on their way. We can all provide words that are deeds at various points in our lives, depending on the circumstance.

Prayer: *Dear Lord, help us to be aware of the needs of others, even when they might be too troubled to speak. Help us offer what is needed – whether that be words or actions. Amen.*

Thought for the day: How can I use my words for good today?

Andrew Billings (Alabama, USA)

Persevering

Read Isaiah 43:1–7

'When you pass through the waters, I will be with you; and when you pass through the rivers, they will not sweep over you.'
Isaiah 43:2 (NIV)

My front window overlooks a pond, where I enjoy watching geese gather. They swim in the rain, waddle across the ice when the pond freezes, and sleep in the water and on the ice.

One winter afternoon, I noticed a goose struggling to move through a shallow layer of ice. She had only a few yards left before she could break free and join her flock. I could not see her feet below the ice, only her neck straining forward. As she moved ahead, the ice closed around her. She looked stuck. I watched, fascinated by her struggle and willing her forward. At last, she broke free and swam easily to join her flock.

Her efforts reminded me of the many times I could see the goal ahead of me yet struggled to get there. I thought of my last semester of graduate school. Though it was only months, graduation seemed years away. Tests and papers stood between me and the day I could break free and join others in my new profession. Throughout that semester, I clung to the words in the scripture above. With God's gift of perseverance, I made it through – just like the goose in icy waters.

Prayer: *Dear God, no matter how frozen or stuck we feel, remind us of your love. Thank you for all you provide, including perseverance in difficult circumstances. Amen.*

Thought for the day: God is greater than my circumstances.

Vicki Krehbiel (Missouri, USA)

A new thing

Read Psalm 104:14–23

'See, I am doing a new thing! Now it springs up; do you not perceive it?'
Isaiah 43:19 (NIV)

Recently, I read Isaiah 43:19 again and was surprised that God had to ask the Israelites, 'Do you not perceive it?' How can God be doing a new thing and it not be perceived? Having worked as a gardener for several years, images of gardens that were overgrown and left unattended came to mind. If a garden is neglected, the grass grows too high; nettles, thistles and other weeds take over where flowers once thrived; trees are never pruned, taking up too much space. A new flowering plant would be difficult to see in such a garden!

Similarly, when our lives are overgrown with relationship troubles, money worries, ill health and other problems, it can be difficult to see the new thing God is doing. Sometimes we need help to see that God is indeed at work in our lives. Jesus describes God as a gardener in John 15:1–2. Sometimes we need God to trim our excessive spending and sort out thorny financial problems, to dig out the roots of our bad habits and prune our tendency to talk unfairly about others. When we focus on Jesus, we can more clearly see the work that God is doing in our lives.

Prayer: *Dear heavenly Father, thank you for caring for us. Help us to see the new thing you are doing in our lives. Amen.*

Thought for the day: God is at work in my life.

Lee Watson (England, United Kingdom)

Finding peace

Read 1 Peter 5:8–11

Philip said, 'Lord, show us the Father and that will be enough for us.'
John 14:8 (NIV)

Soon after my family and I moved to Kansas, where our relatives lived, my grandma – 'Nanny' – passed away. My mum, brother and I had been driving on rural roads when we received the news. I remember trying to comfort my brother and hearing the pain in my mum's screams as she walked down the dirt road.

We stayed in the countryside for hours, and my repeated plea was for God to bring Nanny back to life. I could not believe she was gone. I was furious with God. I didn't want to talk to anyone because no words could possibly be helpful or ease the heartache. I was in a dark place and felt like I had no need for God.

But my grandmother's example reminded me to lean into the comforting arms of Jesus as I mourned her passing. Nanny demonstrated God's love throughout my life and was an amazing example to everyone around her. It was a gift from God that I got to spend part of my life with her.

When I finally prayed, thanking God for putting Nanny in my life and for letting us see her a few more times before she passed, I felt peace in my heart. God gave me understanding and acceptance, and I was able to see past my own desires and trust God's plan. Even though I was still heartbroken, I knew God was with me.

Prayer: *Dear Father, help us to look to you when we are downcast. Give us strength and the peace of your comforting embrace. In Jesus' name. Amen.*

Thought for the day: God will comfort me in my heartache.

Landree DeLee Wedel (Kansas, USA)

God's messenger

Read Colossians 3:12–17

If you utter what is precious and not what is worthless, you shall serve as my mouth.
Jeremiah 15:19 (NRSV)

I try to serve God in as many ways as possible – in my church, in my neighbourhood and through my work. I teach English at a Christian secondary school, and I lead a weekly devotional time for the 13- and 14-year-old students. We read a few verses from the Bible and then discuss them. I ask open-ended questions, and I try to draw the students closer to the Bible story by connecting ordinary examples from our lives to the verses.

I do my best to share my faith and God's love with the students. I talk about my faith experiences, but sometimes I feel that the message is too personal. I want to speak about God's love, not about my feelings and problems. Before I lead each devotional time, I pray, 'Lord, what do you want me to talk about? What is your message to these students today?' I want to humbly share God's message and bless these 70 young people through my words.

As I lead the devotional time, I always feel that the Holy Spirit is with us. I see how carefully the students listen. I pray that God's message reaches and touches their hearts. I am not afraid to talk anymore because the Lord leads my heart, mind and lips. I am happy and honoured to be God's messenger to the children of our school.

Prayer: *Dear heavenly Father, thank you for your love for us. Give us strength and courage to work and speak in your name. Amen.*

Thought for the day: What message does God want me to share today?

Anikó Kovács-Csapó (Hódmezővásárhely, Hungary)

Always welcome

Read Psalm 36:5–12

How precious is your steadfast love, O God! All people may take refuge in the shadow of your wings.
Psalm 36:7 (NRSV)

We adopted our cat Henrietta from a local animal shelter. Our previous beloved cat had died, and we were excited to bring home a new pet. As we walked around the shelter looking at the cats, Henrietta reached her paw out of her cage to me as if to say, 'Save me!' How could I not choose her? However, Henrietta is not the best-behaved cat. She ignores my commands, does whatever she wants whenever she wants to, and refuses to sit in my lap to receive affection from me. Still, I feed and care for her. I love her and welcome her into my arms whenever she decides to come to me.

It occurred to me that Henrietta treats me the same way I sometimes treat God. I sometimes ignore God's teachings, do what I want instead of what God wants me to do, and I try to do things myself instead of allowing God to help me, love me and show me the way. I am sure God loves me immeasurably more than I love Henrietta. If I can welcome back my disobedient cat with so much love, I know God will always welcome me back and forgive me.

Prayer: *Faithful God, thank you for loving us and waiting patiently to show us your constant love. Amen.*

Thought for the day: No matter how often I ignore God, God always welcomes me back.

Gwen Spiess (Texas, USA)

A kind word

Read Luke 10:25–37

A gentle answer turns away wrath, but a harsh word stirs up anger.
Proverbs 15:1 (NIV)

My granddaughter, Gaby, was studying for her driving test, though she was ambivalent about it. I kept encouraging her to consider the fact that she would soon begin classes at university and be starting a new job. Being able to drive would be to her advantage. She finally decided to take the test.

Immediately upon arriving at the station, the staff person told Gaby brusquely he did not have time to administer the test that day and for her to return another time. Undaunted, my granddaughter replied without annoyance that it was quite necessary to get the license on that day for official identification purposes. Still a bit surly, he finally acquiesced.

When she finished the test, he announced in his same manner, 'Okay, you passed.' As she was leaving, she turned to him and said, 'Have a great day.' He made no comment and remained silent as she left. When my granddaughter told me about her experience, I commented that she should have taken a firmer tone in her interaction with that person. But she responded, 'No, Papi, a person with an unpleasant attitude should be treated with common courtesy and a kinder attitude.' The words of Proverbs 15 came to mind as I reflected on Gaby's experience and, more importantly, how she handled it. What a wise lesson she taught me!

Prayer: *O Lord, may our words be acceptable to you and our actions be true to your commandment to love one another. Amen.*

Thought for the day: The Lord rejoices in my kind words and actions towards others.

Edward Rivera Santiago (Puerto Rico)

Answered prayers

Read Psalm 66:16–20

Praise be to God, who has not rejected my prayer or withheld his love from me!

Psalm 66:20 (NIV)

As the caller told me I did not get the teaching job, I felt discouraged and forgotten. My two young children attended the school and the head teacher knew me well, so I had been confident I would be hired. I had also prayed continually about this for several days. I felt like God had not heard my prayers. Did God even care?

For three months I cried out to God, asking why my prayer wasn't answered. Then in October, after the school year had already started, I got a call from the principal of the school asking me to teach a year three class. The school was over-subscribed, and they were creating a new class. I took the job.

As the year progressed, I realised God had heard me after all. God had answered my prayer – just not how or when I had expected. God doesn't always give us what we want. But if we wait and trust, God will give us what we need. My first year of teaching was a blessing. Year three was the perfect class for me, and God knew it was what I needed. Since then I have learned to listen, trust and wait on God's answers.

Prayer: *Dear God, thank you for listening to and answering our prayers. You know what we need before we utter a word. You love us and want us to prosper. Help us to trust in you always. Amen.*

Thought for the day: God answers my prayers, though sometimes in unexpected ways.

Cindy Johnson (Alabama, USA)

Jeremiah shoes

Read Jeremiah 32:6–15

I am convinced that neither death nor life… will be able to separate us from the love of God.
Romans 8:38–39 (NIV)

Several years ago, my husband faced a serious operation with a high mortality rate. Before the operation he bought a new pair of shoes as a sign of hope that he would recover from the operation. These became known as his 'Jeremiah shoes'. God told the prophet Jeremiah that the land of Judah would fall to King Nebuchadnezzar of Babylon and the people would be carried into exile. God, however, instructed Jeremiah to buy a field from his cousin as a sign of God's promise that the people of Israel would return to their land.

My husband thankfully survived the operation and has recovered. Purchasing the shoes was his way of symbolising his trust in God – not that the operation's success was thus guaranteed, but rather as a reminder that, regardless of the outcome, as the apostle Paul wrote, 'neither death nor life… will be able to separate us from the love of God' (Romans 8:38–39).

The experience reminded us that our lives are in God's hands, and reflecting on the promise of God's enduring love gave us both such a sense of peace on the day of his operation.

Prayer: *Heavenly Father, thank you for your 'very great and precious promises' (2 Peter 1:4), which you have given to your people. Amen.*

Thought for the day: We have a sure and certain hope in Christ our Saviour.

Elizabeth Ettles (Scotland, United Kingdom)

Few words

Read Psalm 119:105–112

Your word is a lamp for my feet, a light on my path.

Psalm 119:105 (NIV)

When I was a teenager, during summer holidays I worked at a large house, trimming extensive hedges, cutting the lawns and watering plants in the numerous flower beds. The house was managed by three retired schoolteachers. My afternoons were punctuated with stops for tea and homemade cake.

When I eventually stopped working there, their parting gift to me included a large illustrated Bible – leather bound with gold-leaf pages and black-and-white pictures. With little said, they gave me the gift. There is a popular saying, 'Preach the gospel at all times. Use words if necessary.' Those saintly women knew how to promote the gospel with few words.

Throughout his ministry, Jesus used words to teach and encourage, but his most memorable teaching required few words. Out of great love, he opened wide his arms on the cross and three days later rose to new life.

It was many years before I appreciated the gift of God's word contained in my leather-bound Bible. By the time I fully embraced the gospel, the three women had passed away. I am reminded that our actions do not always yield immediate results and that God's timing is not ours. But we can trust God to guide us.

Prayer: *Dear God, thank you for the people who encourage our faith. May our words and actions bring others closer to you. Amen.*

Thought for the day: God can use my small acts to make a big difference.

Richard Emblin (England, United Kingdom)

Light of life

Read 1 John 1:5–10

He said, 'I am the light of the world. Whoever follows me will never walk in darkness, but will have the light of life.'
John 8:12 (NIV)

On my first Easter in Greece a friend took me to an Orthodox church for the Holy Saturday nighttime service. Hundreds of people gathered for this important occasion – each bearing a long, white candle. As Resurrection Sunday dawned, the priests began chanting, 'Christos Anesti' or 'Christ is risen,' and passed the 'holy light' from their tapers to the worshippers' candles. Each person then passed the light along and echoed, 'Christ is risen!'

Christ described not only himself as the light of the world; he told his disciples that they too are light (see Matthew 5:14). While still carrying our bright-burning candles, we slowly exited the church and walked back to our homes. What a powerful image of spreading the light of the world through the community! And we are called to share that resurrection hope wherever we go. Easter reminds us that we, who lived in darkness, have seen a great light. May the Son's love shine clearly through us!

Prayer: *Dear God, thank you for the new life we have in Christ. May we follow his guiding light in all that we do. Amen.*

Thought for the day: I am God's light bearer to others.

Deborah Meroff (Maine, USA)

Worldwide sunrise

Read Genesis 1:1–5

God said, 'Let there be light,' and there was light.
Genesis 1:3 (NRSV)

In 1965 I was a US Navy pilot serving aboard an aircraft carrier. I was on a plane that returned to the ship just before sunrise – when that narrowest sliver of light begins to separate the ocean's invisible horizon from the black sky. As I walked from my plane towards the debriefing room, I noticed a group of sailors setting up chairs on the flight deck – normally a bustling scene of people and planes. It suddenly dawned on me that it was Easter morning! Under the direction of our chaplain, the crew was creating a temporary chapel for a sunrise service. The usual ear-splitting flight deck had been transformed into a peaceful sanctuary where a group of Christians worshipped the risen Christ – just as dawn broke over the sea.

As we celebrated the resurrection of Jesus, I was reminded that sunrise is a never-ending event. As the Earth turns, the sun peeks over the horizon – inch by inch, moment by moment, day by day. Although I was experiencing a very private moment, millions of other Christians would witness the same miracle of dawn in their own corner of the world. The sun's daily ritual speaks to Christianity's most fundamental belief: the Lord has risen! God's creation of land, sea, sun and sky serves as the never-ending sunrise experience shared daily around the globe. Each moment is a testament to the risen Christ.

Prayer: *Worldwide God, thank you for being everywhere around this planet Earth that all your children call home. We give you thanks for the risen Christ! Amen.*

Thought for the day: Each dawn God shares love and presence with his worldwide family.

John Alter (Florida, USA)

Clean hearts

Read Romans 3:21–26
*'You are already clean because of the word I have spoken to you.
Remain in me, as I also remain in you.'*
John 15:3–4 (NIV)

My house looks clean. The furniture is nicely arranged and looks present-able; the rooms are ventilated and display a sunny appearance. However, when I sweep the floors and do my weekly cleaning with a dusting cloth, I am surprised by the amount of dust and dirt all around, even though everything looks neat and clean.

I think this is a parallel of the way we think about ourselves or how we want to present ourselves to the world. We believe we are doing right and try to act accordingly, but we are imperfect and often fall short. God knows our innermost thoughts and knows exactly what is in our hearts. In the face of this reality, we would do well to recognise and accept God's sovereignty and mercy incarnate in God's son Jesus Christ, who offers us forgiveness. Jesus reminds us, 'You are already clean because of the word I have spoken to you.' And God rejoices in our clean hearts and spirits. Thanks be to God!

Prayer: *God of all, we are grateful for your Son, Jesus Christ, who has wiped away our sins. Come dwell in our hearts and create in us a clean spirit. May your Holy Spirit continue to inspire us and guard our going out and coming in from this time forth. Amen.*

Thought for the day: With God I can have a pure heart.

Estela Baldeon (Lima, Peru)

Pause, ponder and praise

Read Psalm 104:24–31
Great are the works of the Lord; they are pondered by all who delight in them.
Psalm 111:2 (NIV)

Several years ago, on a sunny afternoon in June, I was walking past a pond near some woods. I've walked past this pond on multiple occasions, but on this particular day, I paused to ponder God's creation. The first thing I heard and saw was a red-winged blackbird making a musical sound while swaying on a cattail reed. Then I observed a mourning dove sitting on a nest in a small sycamore tree that was leaning out over the water. The dove's greyish-brown plumage provided perfect camouflage from predators. On the water's surface, pond lilies crowned with white blossoms and cinnamon fern sheltered a female mallard duck.

As I stood pondering these natural wonders, I marvelled that God created all of them. Each plant and bird were evidence of God's creativity. And the beauty and diversity of creation delighted me and inspired my praise. Taking time to observe God's creation is one way we worship. It pleases God when we pause, ponder and offer praise for all the beauty that surrounds us.

Prayer: *Creator God, thank you for all your wondrous works. Forgive us when we take your beautiful creation for granted. Amen.*

Thought for the day: Taking time to ponder creation inspires me to praise God.

Debra Pierce (Massachusetts, USA)

My Easter miracle

Read Colossians 3:1–11

There is no longer Greek and Jew, circumcised and uncircumcised, barbarian, Scythian, enslaved and free, but Christ is all and in all!
Colossians 3:11 (NRSV)

In 1971 I was 19 years old, wandering the country and trying to figure life out. One day I had hitchhiked and found myself at a rest stop along a lonely stretch of desert highway between Los Angeles, California, and Phoenix, Arizona.

I had moved out on my own at age 17, in part because of parents who seemed more confused about life than I was. That began a journey which took me 3,000 miles from home to that highway rest stop. The next morning I met a carload of young people who invited me to church for Easter worship. On an ordinary day, it would have taken a miracle to break through my fears and excuses. But with the promise of a free meal after church, I eagerly agreed to go.

Their church was different from anything I expected. Young people filled the space, singing with smiles that showed me they knew something about Easter that I did not. More importantly, for the first time I considered that God just might be real and actually care about me. I had been running away all my life; now I couldn't run anymore. It took an amazing chain of miracles to bring me to God. But it was Easter, and on Easter miracles happen!

Prayer: *O God, giver of new life, we thank you for searching out those who are wandering and alone. Use us in your work of bringing the lost ones home. We want to be a part of your miracle work. Amen.*

Thought for the day: On Easter, miracles happen!

Peter Caligiuri (Florida, USA)

More than enough

Read John 6:1–15

Glory to God, who is able to do far beyond all that we could ask or imagine by his power at work within us.
Ephesians 3:20 (CEB)

One year I was helping to organise the Christmas service and celebration at my daughter's school. The past two Christmas celebrations had been online due to the pandemic, and I was excited that my daughter finally would be able to celebrate Christmas with her friends and teachers in person!

However, the planning team was unsure how we would cover the cost of the event. We asked for donations from the students' parents, but we didn't expect much. Many of us were experiencing financial difficulties, and it was hard enough to collect our monthly tutor fee.

In today's scripture reading, Philip and Andrew similarly didn't know what to do when Jesus asked them to feed the great crowd. They did not have enough. I prayed and asked God what to do, and God encouraged me to contact friends and relatives. God touched their hearts so that most of them agreed to help. Much like Jesus did with the loaves and fish, God made the impossible possible in our Christmas preparations. The donations exceeded our expectations. We were able to afford the gathering, and we had money left over to cover the tutor fees for at least four months. God is so good.

Prayer: *Loving God, we thank you for your love and care. May we always remember that we can count on you to help us overcome challenges. Amen.*

Thought for the day: God cares for me and my needs more than I can imagine.

Nancy Duma (Jakarta, Indonesia)

God's familiar voice

Read Isaiah 55:1–11

Listen and come to me; listen, and you will live. I will make an everlasting covenant with you.
Isaiah 55:3 (CEB)

There it was – the sound I waited for each day. 'Red,' a male cardinal, had come for his morning visit. For the past several years, he has stopped by most days for a drink of water and a bath. Like good neighbours do, I became familiar with Red's daily habits, bird calls and songs – I knew his voice. I'm surprised how the sound of his soft, sweet call cuts through television, music, traffic and the chatter both in and outside my head. My slightly impaired hearing never misses a trill – Red and I are on the same frequency. His visits are precious to me.

I'm learning that hearing God's voice is a bit like hearing Red's call. When I listen through the ears of my heart, as I would for the voice of a loved one, God's voice breaks through the clutter of the world to bring truth, clarity and grace. Scripture reminds me that I can know God's voice, though I must listen for it and allow it to become familiar.

Listening is active, focused and thoughtful hearing. We must allow ourselves to be available and receptive. We find a fulfilling life when we actively listen for God's voice in our everyday world.

Prayer: *Dear Lord, thank you for your word that reminds us to listen for your voice. Help us to set aside time daily to treasure your presence. Amen.*

Thought for the day: God is speaking. Am I listening?

Jann Mills (Florida, USA)

Divine detour

Read Psalm 37:3–11

In their hearts humans plan their course, but the Lord establishes their steps.
Proverbs 16:9 (NIV)

My cousin Christine had always desired to study peace-building, but after high school she studied social development instead. Years later, she decided to study peace-building at a university in Nairobi. But when she visited the university's website to apply, she saw a job opening for an assistant registrar. She applied and got the job.

Though it seemed like a detour to her career, Christine joined the university as an employee and helped others become peace ambassadors. Three years later, the university gave her a scholarship for her master's degree in peace-building, and now she has graduated. She intends to work for an organisation that enhances peace in Africa. Christine's journey shows that sometimes unexpected paths can ultimately lead to our fulfilling our desires and being a blessing to others.

Sometimes our initial plans may not unfold exactly as we envision them. But God can use unexpected opportunities and circumstances to lead us towards our true desires and purpose. Christine's story is a reminder to me that God's plans may not always align exactly with our own. But God is always working behind the scenes to guide us towards what is best for us.

Prayer: *Dear God, help us to trust in you even when life seems uncertain. Help us to use unexpected opportunities for your glory. Amen.*

Thought for the day: God blesses me in surprising ways.

Barnet Chokani Phiri (Nairobi, Kenya)

Wells of salvation

Read John 4:1–14

'With joy you will draw from the wells of salvation.'
Isaiah 12:3 (NIV)

Water is necessary for life, and these days we mostly just turn on the tap to get it. But it wasn't always so. Before modern plumbing, much of our water came from springs and wells, and it often required a great deal of effort to collect it – as indeed it still does in some parts of the world.

When I was on holiday recently, I visited a castle where the water supply had to be lifted a long way up. In order to do so, a treadmill had been built. Donkeys were used to power the mill, though at some points in the castle's history prisoners of war would be forced to work the wheel. (The treadmill still functions, but of course is only used for demonstration purposes nowadays.) It took a lot of work, but the end result was the water necessary for life.

I think that obtaining the fullness of life that Jesus promised follows the same principle. In his encounter with the Samaritan woman, Jesus compared the life he offers with drawing water from a well. It's there for us to find, but sometimes it requires effort to 'bring it to the surface', such as through prayer, reading the Bible and celebrating our salvation. The more we read God's word and allow God to speak to us, the more joyful our lives can become.

Prayer: *Lord God, as the Samaritan woman asked of Jesus, we also ask you to give us your living water. Quench our thirst for your salvation. Amen.*

Thought for the day: Jesus invites me to come to him and drink (see John 7:37).

Hilary Hartley (England, United Kingdom)

Living by faith

Read Matthew 5:1–12

'Blessed are you when people insult you, persecute you and falsely say all kinds of evil against you because of me.'
Matthew 5:11 (NIV)

As the daughter of an evangelist, my life was one of constant moving. I attended four different elementary schools, and at one school I was even called 'the transfer student'. Many days when I was walking home, boys would spit on me as they rode their bicycles past me and call out 'Christian fool' as they rode away.

One day on my way home, a woman rushed out of a factory holding a broom and yelled at the boys. I recognised her as a woman who always enthusiastically sang hymns in church. She chased after the boys and ordered them to stop this behaviour. From that day, the boys stopped spitting on me.

As a child I believed in Jesus. But when such things happened I complained to God, wishing I had been raised in a different home. I am now about the same age as the woman who chased the boys, and I am walking the same road as my mother and father – living by faith. I now realise that I came to know Christ due to the very fact that I was the child of a minister. And I am grateful to God.

Prayer: *Loving God, bless the people who are the hands and feet of the Lord Jesus. Strengthen our faith in times when it feels hard to follow you. As Jesus taught us, we pray, 'Father, hallowed be your name, your kingdom come. Give us each day our daily bread. Forgive us our sins, for we also forgive everyone who sins against us. And lead us not into temptation' (Luke 11:2–4). Amen.*

Thought for the day: Even when it is difficult, I will live by faith.

Kyoko Minekawa (Chiba Prefecture, Japan)

Salvaged

Read 2 Corinthians 4:7–18

Therefore we do not lose heart. Though outwardly we are wasting away, yet inwardly we are being renewed day by day.
2 Corinthians 4:16 (NIV)

One evening my wife and I were headed out for dinner for our weekly date night. We were driving on the freeway when the flow of traffic came to an abrupt stop. I glanced into my rearview mirror to see that the car behind me wasn't slowing down, and I braced myself and muttered out loud, 'Oh no!' as the car ran into us.

Thankfully, no one was seriously injured. However, the back of my sports car was banged up. The insurance company told me that my car wasn't worth the amount that it was going to cost to have it fixed. They offered me a cheque for the estimated value of the car and told me that if I got it fixed and continued to drive it that it would have a salvaged title. I accepted the cheque and chose to have my car fixed.

It has been nine years since the accident and my 'salvaged' car still runs like new. When I think of my car being made new, I think of what Jesus has done for me by forgiving me of my sins. The truth is, we are all salvaged. We have all fallen short, but by God's grace we have all been given the opportunity to be made new. God sent Jesus to show us the way to eternal life. May we all follow the one who has offered this amazing gift.

Prayer: *Dear God, we know that we have sinned. Yet, you continue to be merciful to us and call us your children. Give us a desire to follow your will for our lives. Amen.*

Thought for the day: God restores me and makes me new.

Rodney Hoven (California, USA)

A cheerful heart

Read 1 Thessalonians 5:16–24

A cheerful heart is good medicine, but a crushed spirit dries up the bones.
Proverbs 17:22 (NIV)

I began noticing a distinct link between the condition of my heart and mind and the condition of my physical body. When stressed, I got headaches. When I was frustrated, my neck and shoulders ached. When I was worried, my heart pounded in my chest, leading to sleepless nights. Not only were negative emotions harming my spirit, but they were functioning as a potent poison to my physical being.

Reading Proverbs 17:22, 'A cheerful heart is good medicine, but a crushed spirit dries up the bones,' I began thinking of ways to have a more cheerful heart. Would a more cheerful heart positively impact my physical body? I asked myself.

I began spending time with God each morning, listing things for which I was grateful. On the drive to work, instead of formulating a to-do list for the office, I listened to praise and worship music. In moments of frustration when it seemed everything was going wrong, I deliberately focused on just one thing going right.

Over time as I embraced these simple new habits, I began to enjoy a more peaceful, grateful and joyful heart. And with that cheerful heart – like the good medicine it is – I felt stronger, healthier and more energised.

Prayer: *Dear God, help us to possess more gratitude in our hearts, exuding thankfulness and joy in all situations. Amen.*

Thought for the day: What is one thing I can do today to adopt a more cheerful heart?

Emily Marszalek (Idaho, USA)

Small group questions

Wednesday 1 January

1 Do you enjoy making New Year's resolutions? Why or why not? How do you usually mark the new year?

2 Why do you think New Year's Eve often feels so exciting? Why do you think the holiday leads many people to reflect on their life and faith journey?

3 Recall your own new beginning with Christ. What was it like? What changes did you observe in yourself as you embraced the Christian faith?

4 In what ways do you continue to grow in faith? How do you know when you are growing in faith? What spiritual practices help you keep growing?

5 How do you prioritise scripture in your daily life? What scripture verses bring you closest to God and most nourish your soul? Why?

Wednesday 8 January

1 When have you or a loved one experienced repeated health challenges? How did you respond to those challenges? How was your faith impacted?

2 Why do you think we tend to doubt or question God in stressful and uncertain times? How are you encouraged by the ways God responds to us in such times?

3 When have you come across a scripture passage that made a big difference for you? What was the passage? Why did it mean so much to you at the time?

4 In what ways do you find peace, comfort and strength in knowing that God is with us no matter what happens? Who or what reminds you of this truth in times when it's easy to lose sight of it?

5   What prayers in scripture do you most relate to right now? Why? How do these prayers encourage you to focus on God?

Wednesday 15 January

1   Do you have a hobby that you have lost touch with? If so, what happened? What hobbies bring you joy today? Why?

2   When have you been asked to serve in a way that made you nervous? How did you respond to the request? What was the outcome?

3   How do you currently serve God and others? In what other ways would you like to serve? How do acts of service deepen your relationships with God and others?

4   Do you have a gift that you are not using to its full capacity? How might you use your gift to serve God more fully? How might you encourage others in your faith community to embrace their own gifts and serve?

5   How are you encouraged to know that any gifts we use to serve God are meaningful? What does it mean to you that God will not judge us on what we bring to serve God?

Wednesday 22 January

1   Recall a time when you were preparing for an important and stressful appointment. What were you thinking? What role did your faith play in that moment?

2   When you desire a certain outcome in a situation, how do you strive to accept God's will? How difficult is it to accept the idea that God's will may be different from your own?

3   When have you received an act of compassion? What do you think led the person to act in that way? How did their act of compassion affect you?

4 How do you remain open to God's power and will? Do you find this easy or difficult to do? What scripture passages and prayers help you remain open?

5 How do you strive to treat others with compassion? Why do you think this is important? How are you inspired to know that God can use our acts of compassion as miracles for others?

Wednesday 29 January

1 When you experience overwhelming grief, do you find yourself questioning God? Why or why not? Who or what helps you continue to trust God even in times of grief?

2 Have you ever received comfort from someone in exactly the way you needed? Describe the situation. What do you think helped that person to know exactly how to comfort you?

3 Do you find it hard to comfort others when you are grieving? When have you struggled to comfort someone? How does your relationship with God help you to comfort others?

4 Do you agree that God can respond to your needs through those around you? Give some examples.

5 Who in your life needs comfort today? How do you sense God nudging you to support them?

Wednesday 5 February

1 When have you done something nice for someone, only to have them respond in a way that felt ungrateful? What did you think or do in response?

2 What most often motivates your acts of kindness? Do you ever do nice things because of what you expect to get in return? Why is it so easy for us to slip into this mindset?

3 Do you find it difficult to love when love and kindness are not reciprocated? Why or why not? What spiritual practices help you love even when it feels difficult?

4 What scripture passages remind you of the importance of loving others as God loves us? How do you remind yourself of these verses when you are struggling to love?

5 How does Jesus' sacrificial love inspire you to love others? How do you strive to follow Jesus' example of love and kindness each day?

Wednesday 12 February

1 What is your dream job? Is it your current job or are you doing something else instead? How do you feel about your job?

2 Do you find it easy to lose sight of the blessings in your life? Why or why not? How do you remain focused on the blessings during the day-to-day busyness?

3 Describe a gratitude practice that has been meaningful for you. Why do you think this practice makes a difference for you? How do you maintain this practice even when you have a lot on your plate?

4 Why do you think it is easy to forget our blessings when we feel worn down? How do your church community and your loved ones help you remain grateful and focused on God even when you are overwhelmed?

5 What blessings are you most grateful for today? Why? How have you expressed your gratitude to God?

Wednesday 19 February

1 When have you been surprised by someone's humble service? Why were you surprised? What did you learn from their example?

2 Describe a time when you had the opportunity to serve others with humility. What did you do? What was the experience like?

3 Why do you think it is common for society to imply that we find happiness in being served? Have you found that to be true? How have you found happiness in serving?

4 Do you tend to agree with Jesus' teaching on serving without putting it into practice? Why or why not? How does your understanding of the teaching change when you actually practise it?

5 Whom can you serve in your community? How will you put Jesus' teaching into practice today? What joy do you think you will experience in doing so?

Wednesday 26 February

1 Were you ever chosen last for games as a child? If so, what was that like? If not, when else were you chosen last?

2 Why do you think it is easy to judge others without knowing their full story? Why does knowing more about someone often make us more merciful and compassionate towards them?

3 Recall a time when you judged or criticised someone, only later to learn that they were going through something difficult. Did your perception of them change? What did you learn through that situation?

4 In what ways do you see others like 'trees walking around'? How does your relationship with Christ help you view others with compassion and love?

5 How do you think Jesus saw people? What does seeing people as Jesus did mean to you? What helps you view others in this way?

Wednesday 5 March

1 Do you find that you derive more benefit from something that you have put a lot of effort into? Give an example from your own experience that supports your answer.

2 Today's writer says, 'Simply going to church isn't enough to build my faith.' Do you agree? Why or why not?

3 The writer mentions several ways that he 'exercises' his faith. Name some other ways that we can exercise our faith. What happens when we don't exercise our faith regularly?

4 Is maintaining a daily spiritual discipline something that is easy or difficult for you? Do you think having a daily discipline is important? Why or why not?

5 When have you experienced the most growth in your Christian faith? When have you struggled to grow spiritually? What would you say to someone struggling to grow spiritually right now?

Wednesday 12 March

1 Describe your relationship with prayer. When is prayer an emotional experience for you? In what circumstances do you find it most difficult to pray?

2 Do you think there are right and wrong ways to pray? Why or why not?

3 What are your favourite prayers in scripture? Why are they your favourite? What have they taught you about prayer?

4 When have you either had or witnessed an experience similar to what the writer describes? Is there ever a time when it is not okay to show our emotions during a worship service?

5 Is praying in public easy or challenging for you? When have you been nervous to pray in front of others? In what kinds of situations are you most comfortable praying?

Wednesday 19 March

1   What does your church building look like? What do you think your building says about your congregation? What do you think it says to people in your community who have never been to church before?

2   When have you experienced church in a 'nontraditional' setting? What did this teach you about church?

3   Do you think it's important for Christian communities to have a designated and consistent space for worship? Why or why not? What might some of the advantages be of meeting in different places?

4   Describe a time when you were in a sacred space that was not a church building. Where were you? What made it sacred?

5   What do you think the church will look like in the future? What do you hope it looks like? What do you think God hopes it will look like?

Wednesday 26 March

1   How do you remind yourself of the gifts God has given you and the ways God has blessed you? How do you show your gratitude for these gifts and blessings?

2   When have you been astounded to see the way God answered one of your prayers? What did this teach you about prayer? What did it teach you about God?

3   How have the ways you serve God changed over the course of your life? Why have they changed?

4   When are you most aware of God's presence? What encouragement would you give to someone struggling to sense God's presence right now?

5   Name a time when you were blessed by the gift of someone's service to God. What gift is God calling you to use in service to others today?

Wednesday 2 April

1 What do you think is your biggest weakness? What is your biggest strength? How do you think God wants us to use our strengths despite our weaknesses?

2 Why do you think God sometimes calls us to tasks for which we feel ill-equipped and inadequate? What can this teach us about God? What can it teach us about ourselves?

3 When have you seen someone use their strengths and their weaknesses to glorify God? How does this inspire you in the work that God is calling you to do?

4 The writer names several people from scripture who felt inadequate but whom God called anyway. Who else in the Bible struggled against feelings of inadequacy? Whose story do you relate to the most? Why?

5 What does it look like to give God our weaknesses as well as our strengths? How does God help us use both our weaknesses and our strengths to serve others?

Wednesday 9 April

1 When has someone offered you comfort in a tense situation through their words? What did this teach you about the power of words? How did it change the way you use words to comfort others?

2 Today's writer says, 'Sometimes we underestimate the power of words, thinking only our actions matter in God's eyes.' Do you think this is true? Why or why not?

3 Have you ever been in a situation in which your words and your deeds became one and the same? In what ways was your experience similar to the writer's? In what ways was it different?

4 When have you remained silent only to wish later that you had spoken up? How did this change the way you use words?

5 To whom can you offer uplifting and life-giving words today?

Wednesday 16 April

1 How can we be confident that God hears our prayers? When have you prayed for something over and over again, but God remained silent? Why do you think God remained silent?

2 When has God answered one of your prayers in an unexpected way? What did this teach you about prayer?

3 Why do you think God's timing is sometimes different from our own? When has waiting on God's timing been frustrating for you? When has it been a blessing?

4 Do you agree that God knows what we need before we ask for it? Why or why not? If God does know what we need before we ask, what is the purpose of prayer?

5 When have you felt that God didn't care about your situation only to discover that God was preparing something for you far better than you could have imagined? What would you say to someone today who feels that God doesn't care about them?

Wednesday 23 April

1 What are some of your earliest memories of church? Did you grow up in church or begin attending later in life? Why is it important for Christians to be part of a church community?

2 Describe your spiritual journey over the course of your life. In what ways has it been like that of today's writer? How has it been different?

3 How do you welcome newcomers into your church community? How do you make them feel at home and know that you care about them? What do you hope they see in your church?

4 Name some ways that your church could be more welcoming to visitors. What will you do to make your church more inviting and hospitable?

5 What Easter miracle are your praying for today? In what ways can you help God make this miracle happen?

Wednesday 30 April

1 How often do you notice a connection between your emotions and the condition of your physical health? Why do you think one can easily affect the other?

2 When have you struggled to find joy in a situation? What do you think God wants us to do when we are having a hard time being joyful?

3 Today's writer mentions several activities that help her deal with stress and have a more cheerful heart. What would you add to this list? What is the one thing you must do each day to feel well mentally and physically?

4 Name some other scripture passages that speak about the connection between our mental and physical selves. Which of these is your favourite? Why?

5 What is causing you stress and worry today? How can your church community pray for you? How can it support you in other ways?

Journal page

Journal page

Journal page

Become a Friend of BRF Ministries
and give regularly to support our ministry

We help people of all ages to grow in faith

We encourage and support individual Christians and churches as they serve and resource the changing spiritual needs of communities today.

Through **Anna Chaplaincy**
we're enabling churches to provide
spiritual care to older people

Through **Living Faith**
we're nurturing faith and resourcing
lifelong discipleship

Through **Messy Church**
we're helping churches to reach out
to families

Through **Parenting for Faith**
we're supporting parents as they raise
their children in the Christian faith

Our ministry is only possible because of the generous support of individuals, churches, trusts and gifts in wills.

As we look to the future and make plans, **regular donations make a huge difference** in ensuring we can both start and finish projects well.

By becoming a Friend and giving regularly to our ministry, you are partnering with us in the gospel and helping change lives.

How your gift makes a difference

£2 a month — Helps us to give away **Living Faith** resources via food banks and chaplaincy services

£10 a month — Helps us to support parents and churches running the **Parenting for Faith** course

£5 a month — Helps us to support **Messy Church** volunteers and grow the wider network

£20 a month — Helps us to develop the reach of **Anna Chaplaincy** and improve spiritual care for older people

How to become a Friend of BRF Ministries

Online – set up a Direct Debit donation at **brf.org.uk/donate** or find out how to set up a Standing Order at **brf.org.uk/friends**

By post – complete and return the form opposite to 'Freepost BRF' (*no other address or stamp is needed*)

If you have any questions, or if you want to change your regular donation or stop giving in the future, do get in touch.

Contact the fundraising team

Email: **giving@brf.org.uk**
Tel: +44 (0)1235 462305
Post: Fundraising team, BRF Ministries,
          15 The Chambers, Vineyard,
          Abingdon OX14 3FE

Registered with

FR

FUNDRAISING
REGULATOR

SHARING OUR VISION – MAKING A GIFT

I would like to make a donation to support BRF Ministries.
Please use my gift for:

☐ Where it is most needed ☐ Anna Chaplaincy ☐ Living Faith
☐ Messy Church ☐ Parenting for Faith

Title	First name/initials	Surname	
Address			
			Postcode
Email			
Telephone			
Signature			Date

Please accept my gift of:

☐ £2 ☐ £5 ☐ £10 ☐ £20 Other £ [＿＿＿＿＿]

by (*delete as appropriate*):

☐ Cheque/Charity Voucher payable to 'BRF'
☐ MasterCard/Visa/Debit card/Charity card

Name on card

Card no. [＿][＿][＿][＿] [＿][＿][＿][＿] [＿][＿][＿][＿] [＿][＿][＿][＿]

Expires end [M][M] [Y][Y] Security code* [＿][＿][＿] *Last 3 digits on the reverse of the card

Signature	Date

Please complete other side of this form

BRF Ministries Gift Aid Declaration
In order to Gift Aid your donation, you must tick the box below.

☐ I want to Gift Aid my donation and any donation I make in the future or
have made in the past four years to BRF Ministries

I am a UK taxpayer and understand that if I pay less Income Tax and/or
Capital Gains Tax in the current tax year than the amount of Gift Aid claimed
on all my donations, it is my responsibility to pay any difference.

Please notify BRF Ministries if you want to cancel this Gift Aid declaration, change
your name or home address, or no longer pay sufficient tax on your income and/or
capital gains.

You can also give online at **brf.org.uk/donate**, which reduces our administra-
tion costs, making your donation go further.

Our ministry is only possible because of the generous support of individuals,
churches, trusts and gifts in wills.

☐ I would like to leave a gift to BRF Ministries in my will.
   Please send me further information.

☐ I would like to find out about giving a regular gift to BRF Ministries.

For help or advice regarding making a gift, please contact
our fundraising team +44 (0)1235 462305

Your privacy

We will use your personal data to process this transaction.
From time to time we may send you information about the
work of BRF Ministries that we think may be of interest to
you. Our privacy policy is available at **brf.org.uk/privacy**.
Please contact us if you wish to discuss your mailing
preferences.

Registered with

FUNDRAISING
REGULATOR

 Please complete other side of this form

Please return this form to 'Freepost BRF'
No other address information or stamp is needed

Bible Reading Fellowship is a charity (233280) and company limited by guarantee (301324),
registered in England and Wales

UR0125

Explore the profound meaning of Easter beyond personal spirituality. There is no doubt that each of us has a place in the Easter story, but what happened on the cross is not just a story of me and Jesus. It is far deeper and wider than that. In this Lenten journey, Jo Swinney explores the broader impact of the Easter story on God's relationship with creation. Through Bible readings, reflections and stories from A Rocha's global conservation efforts, discover how the cross transforms not just our own individual connection with Jesus, but also our relationships with each other and our world.

The Whole Easter Story (BRF Lent book)
Why the cross is good news for all creation
Jo Swinney
978 1 80039 269 4 £9.99
brfonline.org.uk

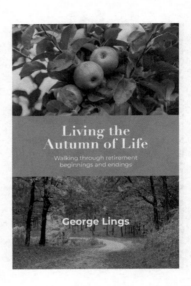

How can we best approach the season between retiring and becoming dependent? Autumn is a time of gains and losses: fruit being harvested and leaves falling. This book charts the experience of living through both realities, drawn from the author's own life and from the views of interviewees. Informed by historical and contemporary reading, it offers snapshots of later life, taken against a backdrop of ageism in society and church. George Lings reflects on the identity of the 'active elderly', and considers through a biblical lens the challenges and opportunities that this season brings.

Living the Autumn of Life
Walking through retirement beginnings and endings
George Lings
978 1 80039 281 6 £12.99
brfonline.org.uk

How to encourage Bible reading in your church

BRF Ministries has been helping individuals connect with the Bible for over 100 years. We want to support churches as they seek to encourage church members into regular Bible reading.

Order a Bible reading resources pack

This pack is designed to give your church the tools to publicise our Bible reading notes. It includes:

- Sample Bible reading notes for your congregation to try.
- Publicity resources, including a poster.
- A church magazine feature about Bible reading notes.

The pack is free, but we welcome a £5 donation to cover the cost of postage. If you require a pack to be sent outside the UK or require a specific number of sample Bible reading notes, please contact us for postage costs. For more information about what the current pack contains, go to **brfonline.org.uk/pages/bible-reading-resources-pack**.

How to order and find out more

- Email **enquiries@brf.org.uk**
- Phone us on +44 (0)1865 319700 Mon–Fri 9.30–17.00.
- Write to us at BRF Ministries, 15 The Chambers, Vineyard, Abingdon OX14 3FE.

Keep informed about our latest initiatives

We are continuing to develop resources to help churches encourage people into regular Bible reading, wherever they are on their journey. Join our email list at **brfonline.org.uk/signup** to stay informed about the latest initiatives that your church could benefit from.

Subscriptions

The Upper Room is published in January, May and September.

Individual subscriptions
The subscription rate for orders for 4 or fewer copies includes postage and packing:

The Upper Room annual individual subscription   £21.30

Group subscriptions
Orders for 5 copies or more, sent to ONE address, are post free:
The Upper Room annual group subscription   £15.75

Please do not send payment with order for a group subscription. We will send an invoice with your first order.

Please note that the annual billing period for group subscriptions runs from 1 May to 30 April.

Copies of the notes may also be obtained from Christian bookshops.

Single copies of *The Upper Room* cost £5.25.

Prices valid until 30 April 2026.

Giant print version
The Upper Room is available in giant print for the visually impaired, from:

Torch Trust for the Blind
Torch House
Torch Way
Northampton Road
Market Harborough
LE16 9HL

Tel: +44 (0)1858 438260
torchtrust.org

THE UPPER ROOM: INDIVIDUAL/GIFT SUBSCRIPTION FORM

To set up a recurring subscription, please go to brfonline.org.uk/ur-subscription

☐ I would like to take out a subscription myself (complete your name and address details once)

☐ I would like to give a gift subscription (please provide both names and addresses)

Title .... First name/initials .... Surname ....

Address ....

.... Postcode ....

Telephone .... Email ....

Gift subscription name ....

Gift subscription address ....

.... Postcode ....

Gift message (20 words max. or include your own gift card):

....

....

Please send *The Upper Room* beginning with the May 2025 / September 2025 / January 2026 issue (*delete as appropriate*):

Annual individual subscription ☐ £21.30

Optional donation* to support the work of BRF Ministries £ ....

Total enclosed £ .... (cheques should be made payable to 'BRF')

*Please complete and return the Gift Aid declaration on page 159 to make your donation even more valuable to us.

Method of payment

Please charge my MasterCard / Visa with £ ....

Card no. ☐☐☐☐ ☐☐☐☐ ☐☐☐☐ ☐☐☐☐

Expires end ☐M☐M ☐Y☐Y   Security code ☐☐☐   Last 3 digits on the reverse of the card

**To set up a recurring subscription, please go to
brfonline.org.uk/ur-subscription**

☐ Please send me .... copies of *The Upper Room* May 2025 /
September 2025 / January 2026 issue (*delete as appropriate*)

Title .... First name/initials .... Surname ....

Address ....

.... Postcode ....

Telephone .... Email ....

Please do not send payment with this order. We will send an invoice with
your first order.

Christian bookshops: All good Christian bookshops stock our resources.
For your nearest stockist, please contact us.

Telephone: The BRF office is open Mon–Fri 9.30–17.00. To place your order,
telephone +44 (0)1865 319700.

Online: brfonline.org.uk/group-subscriptions

☐ Please send me a Bible reading resources pack to encourage Bible
reading in my church

Please return this form with the appropriate payment to:
BRF Ministries, 15 The Chambers, Vineyard, Abingdon OX14 3FE

For terms and cancellation information, please visit **brfonline.org.uk/terms**.

Bible Reading Fellowship is a charity (233280) and company limited by guarantee (301324),
registered in England and Wales

UR0125